Survivors Anonymous

A Structured Guide for recovering from Complex Trauma

A trauma-informed recovery pathway for survivors of abuse and coercive control.

By Tania Brown

Forged in Fire Press

First Edition

Published by
FORGED IN FIRE PRESS
Queensland, Australia

Disclaimer

This book is intended for informational and educational purposes only.

It is not a substitute for professional medical, psychological, or legal advice. The content is based on personal experience, professional insight, and trauma-informed principles, and is designed to support reflection, understanding, and recovery.

Readers are encouraged to seek support from qualified professionals where appropriate.

Content Notice

This book discusses themes including domestic and family violence, trauma, and abuse. Some readers may find certain content distressing. Please engage with the material at your own pace and prioritise your wellbeing.

ISBN: 978-1-7646468-0-2

DEDICATION

For those who survived what should never have happened and are still here— finding their way back to themselves.

To my Mum, Debbie, who above all else has always demonstrated resilience despite the circumstances,

To my uncle Andrew, who has always demonstrated integrity despite the circumstances,

&

To Peter, who helped me return to myself.

Contents

PART I: FOUNDATIONS

CHAPTER 1

Introduction

Survivors Anonymous: A New Way to Heal

I never set out to write a book like this. I set out to survive.

Like many of us, I learned how to keep going long before I ever learned how to live.

I learned how to read a room before I understood my own feelings. How to sense tension before a word was spoken. How to adjust myself—quietly, quickly—to keep things from escalating. I became skilled at shrinking. At softening my voice. At choosing my words carefully. At staying silent when something didn't feel right.

I wore masks so well that, for a long time, I didn't realise I was wearing them at all.

"I'm fine" became automatic. Not just something I said to other people— something I started to believe. And when I couldn't believe it, I learned how to override it.

Push it down. Move past it. Keep going. Because for a long time, that's all I knew how to do. Then one day, the weight of everything I had been carrying caught up with me.

Not all at once. Not in a single dramatic moment. But in the quiet ways things begin to break.

The exhaustion that doesn't go away with sleep. The tension that never fully leaves your body. The sense that something isn't right— even when everything looks fine from the outside.

It builds slowly.

Until one day, you realise you're not just tired. You're holding something that was never meant to be carried this long.

And your body knows it, even if your mind hasn't caught up yet.

What followed wasn't a clean turning point.

It was messy. Disorienting. Painful in ways I didn't yet have language for.

There were moments of clarity— followed by moments of collapse. Moments where I thought, "Okay, I can do this." And others where everything felt too heavy to even begin. But within all of that… something else was there too. Something quieter.

A part of me that hadn't disappeared. A part that was still paying attention. Still noticing. Still holding on. I didn't know it at the time, but that part of me would become the beginning of everything that followed.

I found my way into recovery through the 12 Steps of Alcoholics Anonymous.

Not because I felt ready. Not because I fully understood what I was walking into.

But because something in me had reached a point where continuing the way I was, was no longer possible. I was desperate. I couldn't go on. I was on the brink of total and utter collapse, and suicide was looking more and more appealing. And that was terrifying.

I remember sitting in those rooms for the first time. Not speaking. Not making eye contact. Arms crossed, body tense, trying to appear unaffected.

But listening.

Listening to people say things out loud that I had only ever thought in silence. Things about pain. About shame. About trying to hold everything together while slowly falling apart inside.

And something shifted. Not all at once. Not dramatically.

But enough.

Enough to realise I wasn't the only one who felt like this. I wasn't the only one who had learned to survive this way. And maybe—just maybe— there was a way out of it.

Slowly, something else became clear. I wasn't just recovering from alcohol. Alcohol had been the surface. Underneath it was something much deeper. I was recovering from abuse. From trauma. From years of not feeling safe. From years of learning that my needs didn't matter. From the quiet, persistent belief that I was the problem.

That realisation didn't come gently. It came in pieces. In moments where something I heard landed a little too close. In the discomfort of recognising patterns I hadn't been able to name before. In the slow, confronting awareness that what happened to me had an impact. And that impact didn't disappear just because the situation ended.

Because here's something many survivors are never told clearly:

The end of the abuse is not the end of the experience.

It lives on. In your body. In your reactions. In the way you relate to people. In the way you see yourself. In the choices you make— and the ones you struggle to make. And without language for it, it's easy to turn that inward. To believe something is wrong with me. I should be over this. Why can't I just move on?

What I began to understand—slowly, over time—was this: There was nothing wrong with me. There was something that had happened to me. And everything I had done since then had been an attempt to survive it.

But here's the part that changed everything: The strategies that kept me alive were not the same strategies that would help me heal. And no one had ever shown me the difference.

Because while there were spaces to talk about addiction, and spaces to talk about trauma— There was very little that held both. Very little that understood the overlap. The complexity. The way survival patterns don't just disappear when the danger ends.

What I needed didn't fully exist.

So this was born from that gap.

Survivors Anonymous is a recovery pathway for those of us who have lived through things no human should have to live through Domestic and family violence, Childhood trauma, Sexual assault, Emotional abuse, Coercive control, and the many invisible forms of harm that shape a life from the inside out.

This is for anyone who has ever felt like the person they had to become to survive is now the very thing standing in the way of their healing.

Because here is the truth: Your survival strategies were not failures. They were intelligent. Adaptive. Necessary. They kept you alive in environments where you had limited power, limited safety, and limited options. There is nothing shameful about that.

But survival is not where the story ends.

At some point, something begins to shift.

You start to notice: What once protected you... is now exhausting you. What once kept you safe... is now keeping you stuck. And something inside you begins to ask: There has to be more than this.

And there is.

We deserve more than just getting through the day. We deserve peace. We deserve connection. We deserve to feel at home in ourselves. Not occasionally. Not conditionally. But as a way of living.

Survivors Anonymous offers a peer-led, spiritually grounded, strength-based pathway through that shift.

It does not ask you to ignore what happened. It does not ask you to bypass your pain. It does not ask you to become someone else. It offers something different:

A way to understand what happened. A way to make sense of your patterns. A way to move from survival into healing— at your own pace.

This is not therapy. It does not replace professional support.

But it offers something many survivors never receive: A space where you can be witnessed without needing to defend your truth. A space where you can speak honestly without being fixed. A space where you are held— not just heard.

Here, we don't compare pain. We don't compete in suffering. We don't measure whose story is "bad enough."

If you are here, you belong.

Whether you are ready to dive into healing, or simply exhausted from carrying everything on your own— There is a place for you in this work.

And before we go any further, there are a few things you need to know: You are not broken. You are not too much. You are not beyond repair. **You are a survivor.** And your recovery starts here.

CHAPTER 2

Tania's Story – From Survival to Recovery

After it happened, I didn't feel what I thought I would feel.

There was no immediate clarity. No clean sense of *this is wrong* or *this has to end.* There was just a kind of stillness. Not calm, not peace—something closer to shock.

My body knew something had happened. The bruises told the story. I could feel it in the tightness in my chest, in the way my thoughts didn't quite land, in the strange distance between me and everything around me. It was as if I were standing just outside my own life, watching it unfold rather than fully inside it. But my mind didn't catch up straight away. Instead, it did something else. It tried to make it make sense.

I remember thinking, *That escalated. That wasn't okay.* And then, almost immediately, *But maybe... maybe it wasn't what I think it was. Maybe I pushed him too far. Maybe I should have handled that differently. Maybe he didn't mean to hurt me like that.*

That is the part people don't talk about. The moment after something extreme happens—when your body registers danger, but your mind begins negotiating. Because to fully accept what has just happened means everything has to change. And sometimes, that feels more overwhelming than explaining it away.

So I didn't leave. Not immediately. I adjusted.

There wasn't one moment where everything changed. Not in the way people imagine. It didn't happen all at once. It happened slowly, in ways that were easy to explain away at the time.

At first, it didn't look like something was wrong. It looked like connection. Like intensity. Like something meaningful. There were moments that felt exciting, moments that felt close, moments where I believed I had found something real.

And alongside that—almost quietly at first—there were other moments. Subtle ones. A shift in tone. A look that lingered a little too long. A comment that didn't quite sit right, but wasn't enough to question. Not enough to name.

So I didn't name it. I adjusted.

That became the pattern. Something would happen, it wouldn't feel right, but instead of trusting that feeling, I explained it. I minimised it. I rationalised it.

He didn't mean it like that.

I'm probably overthinking.

It's not a big deal.

Each time I did that, something inside me got quieter.

Over time, the adjustments became automatic. I became more aware of him than I was of myself. I watched his moods, his reactions, the subtle shifts that told me whether things were okay or not. Without realising it, I began shaping myself around that awareness—speaking more carefully, avoiding certain topics, trying to keep things calm, stable, contained.

From the outside, nothing looked obviously wrong. There were no clear signs, no visible markers that something was breaking down. But inside, there was a constant tension. A sense of walking on something unsteady. A quiet awareness that I was no longer fully myself.

There were moments where it became clearer — moments where something happened that I couldn't fully explain away. Where behaviour crossed a line, even if I didn't yet have the language for it. In those moments, something in me reacted. A tightening in my chest. A sense of unease. A brief flash of clarity: *This isn't right.*

But those moments didn't hold.

They were followed, almost immediately, by something else—an apology, a shift, a moment of warmth. Just enough to soften what had happened. Just enough to create doubt. And in that space, I would question myself.

That cycle repeated—tension, discomfort, confusion, then relief. Over and over, until it became harder to hold onto what I had felt in the first place. Harder to trust my own perception.

At some point, I stopped asking, *Is this okay?* and started asking, *How do I make this work?*

That is where something fundamental shifts. You are no longer evaluating the situation—you are adapting to it.

I did not recognise it as abuse at the time. There was no clear label I could point to. What I experienced was not always loud or obvious. But it was consistent. And it changed me.

It changed how I thought. I became more self-critical, more uncertain, more likely to question my own reactions. It changed how I felt. Anxiety became familiar. Tension became normal. Calm felt temporary, something that could disappear without warning. It changed how I moved through the world—more careful, more aware, more focused on avoiding conflict than expressing myself.

Eventually, it changed how I saw myself.

There is a particular kind of disorientation that comes from living like this. Where nothing is clearly "wrong," but nothing feels right either. Where you cannot point to a single moment and say, *That is when it became a problem*, but you can feel, deeply, that something has shifted.

When I finally left, I thought that would be the end of it. That once I was out, everything would settle. It didn't.

The nights told a different story. I would lie awake, exhausted but unable to sleep, as flashbacks came without warning. My chest would tighten, my thoughts would spiral, and my body felt as though it was still living inside something I had already escaped.

I struggled to eat. To concentrate. And the voice in my head—the one that told me it was all my fault—grew louder. That is when I started drinking.

It didn't begin as a collapse. It began as relief. A glass of wine to take the edge off, then another, then something stronger. Something that worked.

For a while, it felt like a solution. It slowed my thoughts, softened the intensity, gave me a brief sense of quiet. But like many coping strategies born from pain, it did not stay contained. What began as relief became reliance, and eventually something I needed just to function. I could sleep a full night without waking up screaming bloody murder.

Looking back now, I can see it clearly. Alcohol was not the problem. It was the symptom. What I was trying to manage was everything underneath it—the trauma, the confusion, the loss of self, the constant internal tension.

Eventually, I ran out of ways to hold it together. Alcohol stopped working.

There was a moment—quiet, but undeniable—standing in my bathroom, gripping the edges of the sink, staring at my reflection. I looked exhausted. Hollow. Unrecognisable.

"I can't do this anymore," I said out loud. "I don't even know who this person is."

And for the first time, I meant it.

I found my way into a 12-step meeting not because I felt ready, but because I had no other options.

I remember sitting in my car before going in, hands on the steering wheel, watching. There were small groups of people gathered outside—mostly older men, standing close together, smoking, talking. They didn't look dangerous, but they didn't feel safe either. No man had ever made me feel safe. They were unfamiliar, and for someone whose body had learned to scan for risk, unfamiliar does not feel neutral.

Part of me questioned everything. *What if this isn't safe? What if I'm walking into something I don't understand? What if I'm making things worse?*

At the same time, there was another part of me—quieter, more exhausted—that knew I could not keep living the way I was living. That part did not care what the room looked like. It only knew that something had to change. And I could always just walk out if I didn't like it. I sat there, caught between those two realities. One trying to protect me, the other asking me to take a risk.

Eventually, I opened the car door. Not because I felt safe, but because I was more afraid of staying the same. Inside, I stayed guarded. I sat at the back, arms crossed, watching everything. And then something shifted.

I did not see predators. I saw people. People who looked worn down, who had lived through things, who were trying to hold themselves together. And when they began to speak, I recognised something—not their stories exactly, but the feeling underneath them. I'd been to meetings before, but this one was different. These people I'd never met were verbalising all of my thoughts. How is that even possible??

The pain. The confusion. The attempt to manage something that never quite stayed managed. For the first time, I did not feel crazy. I felt recognised.

I had not come there for trauma. I had come because I could not stop drinking. Even when I desperately wanted to. Even when it made me sick. Even when I knew it was killing me. I'd swear at the start of the day that I'd just not drink for today, and yet, like I was hijacked by something bigger than me, and no sooner had I sworn off alcohol that I'd be doing a mad dash to the bottle shop, sometimes not even waiting until I'd gotten home, and I'd be drinking again. I needed the relief. Nothing else worked.

And in a complicated way, that is what gave me access.

Because while I was a trauma survivor, I had also reached a point where my drinking had crossed a line. It was no longer social or occasional. It had become compulsive, escalating, something I could not control.

That was the doorway. Not trauma. Addiction.

And I can see now that I was "fortunate" in a very specific way. Because there are many survivors who never develop something visible enough to grant them access to structured recovery. They are still suffering, still carrying the impact, still living with the same internal chaos—but without a place to go. I had both—the trauma underneath, and the behaviour that made it undeniable.

At first, I believed I was there to stop drinking. But as I began working the steps, something became clear.

Alcohol was not the root. It was the response. Alcohol was the bus that got me to the meeting. But when I got to the meeting it wasn't about alcohol at all.

What I was actually seeking was relief from everything beneath it—the trauma, the fear, the loss of self, the beliefs I had built to survive. I didn't know how to manage life on life's terms anymore. I'd run out of ideas, and I was running out of time.

Recovery was not immediate. It was not easy. But it was real. I began to peel back the layers I had built, to face what I had buried, to learn how to exist without escaping myself.

Over time, something deeper shifted. I began to heal from the belief that I was not enough, that I was responsible for what had happened to me, that love had to be earned through disappearing.

Now, I sit in rooms with other survivors. Some are shaking. Some are silent. Some do not yet believe they belong there.

And I tell them what I once needed to hear: You are not broken. You are not what happened to you. You do not have to carry this alone.

Survivors Anonymous was born from that space—from the place where truth is spoken, where shame begins to lift, where healing becomes possible in connection.

I am not who I used to be. I am also not who I thought I had to become. I am something else entirely. I am Tania—a survivor, a woman in recovery, a work in progress. Growing stronger, one day at a time. I still make mistakes. Life still gets hard. But I'm still here. Still trying. And finally, I am someone who is free in ways I once thought were impossible.

CHAPTER 3

A Professional's Perspective: Understanding Trauma in Context

By the time most people begin to ask, *"What's wrong with me?"* something has usually been happening for a long time. Not suddenly, and not in a way that can be traced back to a single moment, but gradually—through experiences that shape how you feel, how you respond, and how you move through the world.

In my work with trauma survivors, one truth has revealed itself again and again: the impact of abuse does not end when the abuse stops. It continues—often quietly, often invisibly—in the body, in the nervous system, and in the way a person comes to understand themselves, others, and the world around them. Trauma is not just something we remember. It is something we carry.

For a long time, trauma was misunderstood as something purely psychological—something that could be talked through, managed, or eventually left behind. We now know that this is only part of the picture. Trauma is not just cognitive. It is physiological.

When a person is exposed to ongoing stress, fear, or abuse—especially over time—their nervous system adapts in order to survive. The body learns to stay alert, to scan constantly for danger, to react quickly even when there is no immediate threat. These responses are not chosen. They are automatic.

They are the body doing exactly what it was designed to do: **protect**.

In moments of genuine danger, this system is essential. It sharpens awareness, mobilises energy, and increases the chances of survival. But when these responses are activated repeatedly, or in environments where there is no clear escape, they do not simply switch off when the situation changes. They become embedded.

Over time, the body begins to learn something about the world. It learns that people can be unpredictable, that safety is not guaranteed, and that vigilance is necessary. That learning does not sit neatly in conscious thought. It lives in the body.

You may notice it in ways that are difficult to explain at first. A tension that never fully leaves. A heightened awareness of your surroundings. An instinct to track other people's moods before they are spoken. You begin anticipating rather than responding, adjusting yourself in advance to avoid what might happen.

As these patterns become more established, they begin to shape daily life. You may find yourself reacting strongly to situations that seem minor to others, feeling anxious without a clear reason, or struggling to relax even in environments that are objectively safe. You may replay conversations, question your responses, or feel responsible for how others feel.

These are not random behaviours, and they are not personality flaws. They are learned responses. Your nervous system is doing exactly what it has been trained to do: protect you.

The difficulty is that the nervous system does not always recognise when the danger has passed. It continues to respond as though the conditions that shaped it are still present. This is why trauma can feel so confusing. You may find yourself asking why you are reacting this way, or why something that is "over" still feels active in your body.

The answer is not that you are overreacting. It is that your nervous system is responding not only to the present moment, but to what it has learned from the past.

Survivors often experience this in very real and tangible ways—hypervigilance, where the body is constantly scanning for danger; anxiety or panic that arises even in safe environments; dissociation, where there is a sense of disconnection from self or surroundings; chronic exhaustion from being in a constant state of alert; difficulty trusting others, or even trusting one's own perception; and at times, emotional overwhelm, followed by periods of numbness.

These are not signs of weakness. They are adaptations. They are the body and mind attempting to make sense of something that was never safe to begin with.

Research has reinforced what survivors have long known through lived experience. The Adverse Childhood Experiences (ACE) Study, first conducted in the 1990s, demonstrated a clear relationship between early exposure to adversity—such as abuse, neglect, or household dysfunction—and long-term health outcomes. Individuals with higher levels of early trauma were significantly more likely to experience mental health challenges, addiction, chronic illness, relationship difficulties, and exposure to further violence.

This does not occur because people are broken. It occurs because their systems adapted in order to survive.

Trauma, however, does not exist in isolation. It is shaped by the environments in which it occurs—by family systems, social norms, cultural expectations, and broader structures of power. For many survivors, particularly women, these structures have not always been safe.

To understand abuse in the present, it is necessary to acknowledge the past. For much of history, power imbalances within relationships were not only common, but normalised. Women were treated as property. Children were expected to obey without question. Violence within the home was considered private, not criminal. Even in relatively recent history, marital rape was not recognised as a crime, domestic violence was minimised or ignored, and survivors were frequently blamed, silenced, or disbelieved.

These were not isolated attitudes. They were embedded in legal, cultural, and institutional systems. While much has changed, the echoes of that history continue to shape how abuse is understood—and often misunderstood—today.

Because of this, many survivors have been misdiagnosed, dismissed, or labelled as "too emotional," "difficult," or "unstable." They are often treated for symptoms—panic attacks, substance use, emotional reactivity, chronic pain—without those symptoms being understood in context. What is seen as the problem is, in many cases, the response to the problem.

There is, however, a shift occurring. Slowly, but meaningfully, trauma is being understood differently.

There is increasing recognition that abuse is not about anger, but about **control**; that survivors do not remain in harmful situations because they are weak, but because leaving can be complex and dangerous; and that recovery is not about forgetting what happened, but about integrating the experience and reclaiming a sense of self.

Perhaps most importantly, there is a growing willingness to listen to survivors.

Healing, however, is not something that happens in isolation. Trauma happens when your body registers imminent danger, and by escaping that danger you're left without relational safety. The nervous system gets stuck. It continues to signal DANGER, and the mind scrambles to make sense of the signal, but it can't.

Trauma often occurs in relationship, and recovery must also involve relationship. It happens in spaces where people are believed, where they are not judged, not analysed, not treated as problems to be fixed, but met as human beings with lived experience.

This is where something begins to shift.

Because when a person is no longer alone in their experience—when their reality is acknowledged rather than questioned—the nervous system begins to settle. The mind replays the signal, and the body, when in connection with others, begins to relax. Safety, even in small amounts, creates the conditions for change.

This is where Survivors Anonymous sits.

It is not a clinical model, and it is not a replacement for therapy. It is something many survivors have never had access to: a space where lived experience is honoured, where truth can be spoken without being minimised or challenged, and where people are met as equals rather than as cases to be managed.

It is built on a simple but often overlooked understanding: survivors already carry insight into their own experience. Healing is not something done to them. It is something built with them.

Recovery, then, is not about returning to who you were before trauma. That version of you existed under different conditions.

Recovery is about becoming someone new—someone who understands their patterns, who can regulate their responses, who can set boundaries, trust themselves, and begin to feel safe in their own body again.

Not perfectly. But progressively.

The impact of trauma is real. It is measurable, and it can be profound. But so is the capacity for healing. When the right conditions are present—safety, connection, understanding, and space—something remarkable begins to happen.

People do not simply survive. They begin, piece by piece, to rebuild. And over time, they begin to reclaim their lives.

CHAPTER 4

The Cage Without Bars

Understanding Coercive Control

For a long time, I didn't think I was in an abusive relationship.

There was nothing obvious to point to. No single moment I could hold up and say, *that's it, that's where the line was crossed.*

He didn't hit me in those early stages. He didn't shout in ways that would draw attention. In public, he could be warm, even attentive. He bought me flowers. Paid the bills. Slept beside me at night. From the outside, it didn't look like something was wrong.

And that's part of what made it so hard to see.

Because what was happening wasn't loud. It wasn't immediate. It didn't arrive as something clearly defined.

It unfolded.

Slowly. Quietly. In ways that were easy to explain, easy to dismiss, easy to adapt to.

At first, the changes were small enough that I barely registered them. I stopped laughing the way I used to. I stopped seeing certain friends, not because I was told I couldn't, but because it became easier not to. I began choosing clothes more carefully, aware—without being told—of what might create tension. I started editing myself in conversations, softening opinions, avoiding anything that might shift the mood.

None of it felt like a decision. It felt like adjustment. Over time, something more subtle began to shift.

I stopped trusting my instincts.

There would be moments—small, fleeting—where something didn't feel right. A comment that landed a little too sharply. A reaction that didn't match what had happened. A tension in the air that I couldn't quite explain.

My body would register it first. A tightening. A pause. A quiet sense of unease.

And then my mind would step in.

You're overthinking.
It's not a big deal.
Don't make something out of nothing.

That internal negotiation became constant.

And slowly, almost imperceptibly, I began to move further away from myself.

By the time I realised something was wrong, there were no bruises to point to. Just a quiet, aching loneliness. And a growing sense that I was no longer living my own life.

That is the nature of coercive control.

It is not defined by a single incident. It is defined by a pattern—a pattern of behaviours that work together over time to dominate, isolate, and destabilise another person.

Individually, those behaviours can seem insignificant. Explainable. Even normal.

A question about who you're texting.
A comment about what you're wearing.
A suggestion that a friend isn't good for you.
A moment of withdrawal when you say the "wrong" thing.

Each one, on its own, can be rationalised. But together, over time, they form something else entirely.

A system.

Coercive control operates by shifting the ground beneath you.

Not all at once, but gradually—until what once felt clear becomes uncertain, and what once felt like choice begins to feel like obligation.

You begin to anticipate reactions before they happen. You adjust your behaviour to maintain stability. You become highly attuned to someone else's emotional state, often at the expense of your own.

And in that process, something begins to erode. Not just your circumstances, but your sense of self. You start asking yourself questions you never used to ask.

Am I overreacting?
Did I misunderstand?
Maybe it is my fault.
If I just handled things differently, this wouldn't happen.

Those questions don't arise by accident. They are part of the control. Because when you begin to doubt yourself, you become easier to influence. Easier to manage. Easier to keep within the boundaries someone else has created.

One of the most devastating aspects of coercive control is how difficult it is to recognise, especially from the inside. It often begins with intensity that feels like connection. Attention that feels like care.

Statements that sound like love.

"I just want to be with you all the time. I love you SO much."

"If I can't be with you I can't go on. You mean everything to me."

"I only get jealous because I care."

There is a logic to it that makes it difficult to challenge.

And because much of it happens in private, there are few external reference points. To others, the relationship may appear stable, even ideal. There is no visible evidence of harm.

So you adapt. You normalise. You adjust your behaviour in ways that reduce tension and increase predictability. And without language for what is happening, it becomes increasingly difficult to name. Without naming it, it becomes almost impossible to leave.

Many survivors describe coercive control as confusing, and that confusion is not accidental. Because alongside the harm, there are often moments of kindness. Moments of connection. Moments that feel real. And those moments matter. They create hope. They offer relief. They make it harder to reconcile the harm with the person causing it. But over time, something becomes clear—often quietly, often slowly.

Love does not require fear. Love does not require silence. Love does not require you to shrink yourself in order to keep the peace. If you find yourself constantly managing another person's emotions to stay safe, that is not love.

That is control.

Coercive control does not exist in isolation. It is reinforced by broader systems that have, for a long time, normalised imbalance within relationships.

For generations, control was minimised, dismissed, or reframed as responsibility. Women were expected to accommodate. Children were expected to obey. Silence was often interpreted as strength. These messages do not disappear simply because society begins to change. They continue to shape how behaviour is interpreted—what is tolerated, what is excused, and what is overlooked.

Understanding coercive control, then, is not only about recognising individual relationships. It is about recognising patterns that have been allowed to exist for far too long.

There is often a moment—different for everyone—when something begins to shift.

The confusion starts to clear. The pattern becomes visible. The feeling of *something isn't right* finally finds language. That moment matters.

Because once you can name coercive control, something begins to return.

Your sense of reality. Your voice. Your right to safety. Your connection to yourself. You begin to understand that what happened was not your fault. That your responses made sense. That your instincts were never wrong—you were just taught, slowly and consistently, to ignore them.

Recovery from coercive control is not only about leaving the relationship.

It is about rebuilding what was eroded. Your trust in your own perception. Your ability to make decisions without fear. Your connection to your needs, your boundaries, your sense of self.

This does not happen all at once.

Because the effects of coercive control do not disappear the moment the relationship ends. But something important begins the moment you see it clearly. You stop trying to fix what was never yours to fix.

If you are reading this and recognising parts of your own experience, it is worth pausing for a moment. To notice what is happening in your body. To acknowledge what is coming up. And to hear this clearly:

You are not imagining it.
You are not overreacting.
You are not the problem.

There is nothing wrong with you for not seeing it sooner. There is nothing wrong with you for staying. There is nothing wrong with you for still feeling the impact.

There is a name for what you experienced. And there is a way forward.

Coercive control is often invisible to others. But it is never invisible to the person living inside it. It exists in the tension, in the hesitation, in the quiet adjustments made to keep the peace. It exists in the space between what is said and what is felt.

Naming it does not undo what happened. But it does something just as powerful.

It brings you back to yourself.

CHAPTER 5

What Kept Us Alive - Understanding Survival Responses

When we talk about trauma, we often focus on what happened. The event. The person. The harm. We look for the moment things went wrong, as though understanding that alone will explain everything that followed.

But there is something just as important—something that rarely receives the same attention. What we did to survive it. Because that is where the truth lives.

Every survivor carries a set of responses shaped in moments of danger. Not chosen. Not consciously learned. Not decided through logic or reflection. They emerge automatically, instinctively, through the body's need to protect itself.

These are survival responses—the ways the nervous system adapts when safety is no longer guaranteed. They do not always look the way people expect.

Sometimes they look like strength. Sometimes they look like silence. Sometimes they look like behaviours we later judge ourselves for, without ever asking where they came from. But every one of them had a purpose.

They kept us alive.

In my work, and in my own experience, I have seen how easily these responses are misunderstood. People often interpret them as personality traits, flaws, or failures of character. They ask why someone didn't leave, why they didn't speak up, why they reacted the way they did.

What is often missing from those questions is context. Because in the moment those responses were formed, they were not choices. They were adaptations. The body assessing what was most likely to preserve safety, and acting accordingly.

Most of these responses fall into four broad patterns: fight, flight, freeze, and fawn. These are not rigid categories, and they are not mutually exclusive. Many survivors move between them, depending on what was safest at the time.

The **fight response** is often the most visible, and the most misunderstood. It is commonly associated with anger or aggression, but at its core, fight is about refusing to be powerless.

It is the part of you that says, *I will not be overrun by this.*

For some, this shows up as confrontation or defensiveness. For others, it appears as control—of environment, of outcomes, of self. It can look like hyper-independence, an insistence on not needing anyone, or a drive toward perfectionism where everything must be managed, contained, and correct.

Many people who develop a strong fight response do so because no one protected them. Over time, they become their own protector. There is strength in that. But there is also a cost. To live in a constant state of readiness, always braced, always prepared, is exhausting.

The **flight response** moves in a different direction. Where fight holds ground, flight seeks escape.

It says, *If I can get away, I'll be safe.*

Sometimes this is literal—leaving situations, ending relationships, creating distance. But more often, it becomes internalised. It shows up as constant movement: staying busy, overworking, overachieving, filling every available space so there is no time to feel.

It can look like avoidance of conflict, discomfort with emotional closeness, or a persistent sense of restlessness. For some, it becomes a form of escape through substances, distraction, or anything that creates distance from what is difficult to sit with.

Flight is the nervous system trying to outrun pain. And for a time, it works. Until eventually, the body can no longer keep up.

Then there is the **freeze response**. Freeze is quieter, less visible, and often the most misunderstood of all. It emerges when neither fighting nor fleeing feels possible.

It says, *If I become still, I might survive this.*

This is the shutdown response. The one that protects by disconnecting.

It can look like dissociation, where a person feels detached from their body or surroundings. It can look like numbness, an absence of feeling where something should be. It can appear as an inability to act, speak, or respond in moments of stress, even when there is a desire to do so.

From the outside, it is often interpreted as passivity or weakness.

But freeze is neither. It is the body's last line of defence—an adaptive response that allows a person to endure what cannot be escaped. It protects by dulling sensation, by creating distance, by making the unbearable survivable. That is not failure. That is survival.

The **fawn response** is perhaps the most easily overlooked, because it often looks like compliance, kindness, or cooperation.

At its core, fawn says, *If I keep them happy, I will be safe.*

This response develops in environments where safety depends on maintaining connection. Where conflict increases risk, and attunement to another person's needs becomes the safest path forward.

It can look like people-pleasing, over-apologising, or a deep discomfort with saying no. It may involve prioritising others' needs over your own, taking responsibility for other people's emotions, or adapting yourself in subtle ways to avoid tension.

Fawn is not weakness. It is strategy. It is the nervous system recognising that in certain environments, connection—not resistance—is the safest form of protection.

These responses do not disappear when the environment changes. The body remembers.

Even when the danger has passed, the nervous system continues to respond as though it is still present. This is why you may find yourself reacting strongly to something that seems small, shutting down when nothing is technically wrong, or feeling unsafe in environments that are objectively secure.

It is not because you are broken. It is because your system has been conditioned.

For many survivors, this is where confusion begins to turn inward. Without understanding these responses, it is easy to interpret them as personal failure. To wonder why you cannot "just move on," why you still react, why your body does not align with your circumstances.

But these responses are not evidence that something is wrong with you. They are evidence that something happened *to you*.

In Survivors Anonymous, the goal is not to eliminate these responses or to fight against them. It is to understand them.

To recognise them as they arise. To be able to say, This is my fight response. Or, I'm in flight right now. Or, I've gone into freeze. Or, I'm fawning. And in that moment of recognition, something changes. You are no longer entirely inside the response. You are aware of it.

That awareness creates space. Space between the trigger and the reaction. Space between what is happening now and what has happened before. Space where something new becomes possible.

Choice.

Before anything can change, however, something else must happen first.

Acknowledgment.

These responses worked. They carried you through situations you were never meant to endure. They allowed you to survive when your options were limited, when your power was restricted, and when safety was uncertain.

There is nothing shameful about that. But survival is not the end of the story.

What kept you safe then may not be what you need now.

And this is where recovery begins—not by rejecting these parts of yourself, but by becoming curious about them. By asking, gently and without judgment, *Is this still serving me?*

Healing is not about becoming a different person. It is about becoming a more aware one. We do not get rid of our survival responses. We integrate them.

We learn to recognise when they are activated, to understand what they are trying to protect, and to respond with intention rather than fear. We begin to give ourselves what we did not receive at the time—safety, validation, permission to exist as we are.

Over time, something begins to shift.

The fight softens. The flight slows. The freeze begins to thaw. The fawn starts to find its voice. And gradually, the whole self begins to emerge.

You are not the problem. Your responses are not evidence that something is wrong with you. They are evidence that your system did exactly what it needed to do to survive, and your body is recognising the same lack of safety in that moment.

Now, you have something you did not have then.

Awareness.

Language.

Choice.

And from here, something powerful becomes possible.

Not just survival— but healing.

CHAPTER 6

The Invisible Tie - Understanding Trauma Bonds

By the time I understood what a trauma bond actually was, I was already out of it. But I wasn't free of it. That was the part that stayed with me.

Because nothing about my relationship with Ted looked like something I should have struggled to leave. There was no single moment I could point to and say, *that's where it became dangerous*. There were no obvious markers. No clear escalation. No version of the story that would make immediate sense to someone on the outside.

If anything, it looked like something else entirely. Two people in recovery. Two people who understood pain. Two people trying to build something honest.

That's what made it so difficult to see. Because the harm didn't arrive loudly. It arrived quietly. And it stayed.

There were moments with him that felt real in a way that is hard to explain unless you've experienced it. Not surface-level connection, but something deeper. A sense of being understood. Of being met in places that had previously felt hidden. It created a kind of closeness that doesn't just feel good. It feels meaningful.

And meaning is what binds. It's what makes you stay longer than you should.

But alongside that, there were other moments. Small at first. Easy to miss if you weren't looking directly at them. A shift in tone. A delay that didn't quite make sense. A response that didn't land. Something that felt slightly off, but not enough to fully name. Just enough to feel.

And then, just as that feeling started to settle in, something else would follow. A message. A softness. A return to warmth. And with that, relief.

It's the relief that does it. Not the harm. The relief.

At the time, I didn't have language for what I was experiencing. I only knew that something in me kept leaning in, even when something else was quietly pulling back. I told myself it was connection. That it was just complexity. That it was what happens when two people who have lived through things try to come together.

But underneath that, something else was happening. A pattern was forming.

From a clinical perspective, trauma bonds are built through inconsistency. Not through constant harm, but through the unpredictable cycling between disconnection and reconnection. The nervous system becomes engaged in that cycle. It begins to anticipate the return, to hold on through the discomfort, because it has learned that relief will come. And when it does, it feels earned. That's what makes it so powerful.

With Ted, I began to notice that I was thinking about him more than I was thinking about myself. Not in a way that felt obsessive at first, but in a way that felt orienting. I was tracking the space between interactions. Reading into pauses. Trying to make sense of what wasn't being said.

I adjusted. Quietly. Gradually.

I softened things I would have questioned before. I gave more space than I normally would have. I told myself stories that made the discomfort easier to hold. Not because I didn't trust myself, but because every time something felt off, it was followed by something that made it feel okay again.

That's how the bond holds. It doesn't erase your clarity. It interrupts it.

There were moments where I could feel it clearly. A tightening in my chest. A thought that didn't quite sit right. A flicker of something that said, *this isn't what you think it is.*

But those moments didn't stay. Because something always came after them. Something that softened it. Something that made me question whether I'd imagined it. And slowly, without deciding to, I started to trust those moments less.

This is where something shifts internally. You stop asking, *is this okay?* and you start asking, *how do I make this work?*

From the outside, nothing about this looks extreme. But from the inside, it becomes disorienting. Because you are holding two realities at once. This feels real. This doesn't feel right. And instead of choosing between them, you begin trying to reconcile them. To make both things true.

That reconciliation is what keeps you there.

Because walking away would mean letting go of the part that felt real. The part that mattered. The part that made you believe there was something there worth holding onto.

What I didn't understand at the time was that my body was involved in this far more than my thoughts were. There is a biological component to trauma bonding that people rarely talk about in a way that lands. The cycle of tension and relief activates the same pathways in the brain that are involved in addiction. It creates anticipation. It creates attachment. It creates a pull that doesn't respond to logic.

You are not just thinking your way through it. You are feeling your way through it. And your body is learning, over and over again, to stay.

By the time I began to feel the cost of it, I was already in it. Not trapped. But bound.

And when it ended, the bond didn't end with it. That's what surprised me the most. Because I could see, clearly, that it wasn't right. I could see the pattern. I could see what had happened. And still, there was a pull.

Not toward him, exactly. But toward the feeling of him. The memory of the connection. The version of it I had kept trying to return to.

That's when I understood something important. You don't just leave the person. You have to unwind the pattern.

And for me, that meant going back through it, not to relive it, but to see it. From the moment of repair to the next rupture. Watching it as a sequence instead of a story.

I saw the person I thought loved me, cared about me, wanted the best for me, for who he really was. The person who told me, when I was suicidal, to call Lifeline, as though it was such an inconvenient disclosure that it didn't even warrant engagement. The person who then shamed me for getting drunk and punished me by abusing systems and calling police, while he and the kids went to Cairns for our holiday without me.

I saw him gradually "come around," but only after I profusely apologised for my behaviour and recommitted to my sobriety. And even then, something didn't sit right.

So instead of pushing it down again, I looked. Quietly. Properly.

Everything I had dismissed. Everything I had explained away. Everything I had doubted in myself. I let myself see it.

And that's when the whole thing shifted.

I saw the lack of empathy. The entitlement. The ego. The bravado. The "good dad" persona that never aligned with being a good dad. The seething rage sitting just under the surface. The secrecy. The deception. The double standards. The way he justified things that would have been unacceptable if they had come from anyone else. The judgment. What I noticed most was an overall sense of apathy, a lack of care factor. If there was any care there, it was overshadowed by contempt. Almost a superiority complex.

I recommitted to abstaining from alcohol, and there he was, a "recovered" meth addict using MDMA on a "boys' weekend" while he was meant to be caring for his ten-year-old son. I watched him minimise what he had exposed that child to. I watched him gloat about his doctor "trusting him again" with narcotics.

I watched him preparing a quantity of green leafy matter to "take over to a mate". I watched his excitement when he got strong opioids, never legally, always from “a mate”, the way he justified using them for “back pain” that didn’t exist. I watched how these drugs were mentioned once, and then suddenly never again. And when I asked him about them, he said he took them.

And I watched the panic when he couldn’t find his drugs. I heard the panic as he opened the zippers, and closed them, and opened them again, desperate to locate his precious pills. I watched the anger brewing. I watched the irritation growing. I saw the cravings kick in, and I saw how any minor irritation appeared to have a disproportionate reaction.

Then the rupture again. The accusations. The blame. The projection.

This was a man who was meant to be in recovery. And suddenly, it was all clear. He’d never stopped. It explained the inconsistency, the low mood, the random “sprinkler checks” at night, or “power switch checks” or in the early hours of the morning.

I thought I’d have to watch for erratic behaviour. But when a chronic meth addict uses meth, they don’t present that way. It’s much more covert – it looked like always having to be right, a low tolerance for relational feedback, and a reduced capacity for reflection. It looked like focusing on a task rather than a connection. Conversations feel hollow. Moods shift out of nowhere. Irritability comes to the forefront. And you sit there the whole time wondering *“What’s really going on here?”*

The pull isn't love in the way we're taught to understand it. It's conditioning. It's your system expecting the cycle to complete. Expecting the relief to follow the tension, even when the source of that cycle is no longer present.

When I finally saw it clearly, really saw it, something shifted in a way that didn't require force. Because once you understand the pattern, you can't unsee it. And once you can't unsee it, you are no longer inside it in the same way.

Breaking a trauma bond isn't about willpower. It's about clarity. About stepping out of the cycle long enough for your body to experience something different. Something consistent. Something that doesn't spike and drop. Something that doesn't require you to question yourself. Something steady.

Over time, the intensity fades. Not because it wasn't real, but because it was never stable. And what is left is something much clearer. Not just about them, but about you.

I didn't stay because I was weak. I stayed because I was conditioned. And once I understood that, I stopped trying to go back. Because there was nothing there to return to.

CHAPTER 7

Meeting the Inner Survivor – The Parts of Us That Protected Us

We carry many versions of ourselves inside us, whether we realise it or not. The version that fought back. The version that froze. The one who tried to be perfect. The one who stayed quiet. The one who ran. The one who numbed out. The one who held everything together, and the one who didn't.

Each of these parts has a story. Each one formed in response to something. Each one, in its own way, helped us survive.

After trauma—especially trauma that is repeated, relational, or experienced early in life—it is common to feel as though you are not entirely one, consistent self. Instead, you may feel fragmented, as though different parts of you take over at different times.

There are moments where you respond calmly and clearly, and others where your reactions feel disproportionate, confusing, or out of your control. You may find yourself wondering why something small triggers a strong emotional response, why you suddenly feel like a child in certain situations, or why you move between shutdown and overwhelm without understanding what changed.

It can feel disorienting, even frightening, to experience yourself this way. But this is not instability. It is adaptation.

When you were in situations where you did not have the safety, support, or power to respond freely, your system found other ways to cope. It created different responses—different internal states, or "parts"—that could manage different kinds of danger. Some learned to protect. Some learned to appease. Some learned to disappear. Some learned to carry what could not be processed at the time.

In trauma recovery, this is often understood through what is called parts work. It recognises that we are not a single, fixed identity, but a system made up of different internal parts, each with its own role. Some parts are active and visible, shaping how we think and behave in the present. Others remain in the background, holding memories, emotions, or beliefs that were too overwhelming to process when they were formed.

These parts are not mistakes. They are not evidence that something is wrong with you. They are intelligent responses to experiences that required adaptation in order to survive.

If you begin to look closely, you may recognise some of these parts within yourself. There may be a part of you that is strong, alert, and defensive, quick to react or push back, unwilling to be vulnerable because vulnerability once came at a cost. There may be a part that is deeply attuned to others, always scanning for how people feel, adjusting, accommodating, trying to keep the peace. Another part may be driven and capable, pushing you to achieve, to perform, to prove your worth in ways that feel both productive and exhausting. There may be a part that disconnects entirely when things become too much—numb, distant, difficult to reach.

And somewhere within all of this, there is often a more vulnerable part, carrying grief, fear, or unmet needs from a time when those needs could not be safely expressed. There may also be a part that escapes—through distraction, through substances, through anything that creates distance from what is difficult to feel.

Each of these parts developed for a reason. Each one was trying to help.

And yet, as adults, we often judge them harshly. We ask ourselves why we are like this, why we cannot just be different, why certain patterns keep repeating even when we know they do not serve us. We may feel frustrated with the part that shuts down, angry at the part that pushes people away, or ashamed of the part that seeks comfort in ways we do not fully understand.

But when we look more closely, something important becomes clear.

These parts are not trying to harm us. They are trying to protect us, using the only strategies they know. Even when those strategies no longer serve us, they remain rooted in an original purpose: **survival.**

Healing does not begin with eliminating these parts. It begins with meeting them.

This requires a shift—from judgment to curiosity. Instead of asking what is wrong with you, you begin to ask different questions. When did this part first appear? What was happening at that time? What was it trying to protect you from? What did you need then that you did not receive? And what might that part need now?

This is not about analysing yourself in a detached or clinical way. It is about building a relationship with yourself, one that is grounded in understanding rather than criticism.

Without that understanding, these parts can feel as though they are working against you. One part may want connection, while another pushes people away. One part may want rest, while another demands constant productivity. One part may want to speak, while another shuts everything down. This internal tension can feel like conflict, like something inside you is fractured or at odds with itself.

But when you begin to understand these parts, the conflict starts to make sense. You realise they are not opposing forces—they are different forms of protection, each shaped by different experiences and needs.

And when that understanding deepens, the goal begins to change. It is no longer about controlling or suppressing these parts. It becomes about relating to them with compassion.

Sometimes, that connection can begin in very simple ways. It might look like pausing in a moment of reaction and recognising what is happening internally. It might look like acknowledging a part of you that is scared, or overwhelmed, or trying to keep everything together. It might even take the form of speaking directly to that part, offering it something it has not received before.

Something as simple as, *I see you. I know you were doing your best. I know you were trying to protect me.*

For many people, this is unfamiliar. We are used to pushing parts of ourselves away, not turning toward them. But over time, that shift—from rejection to recognition—begins to change the relationship you have with yourself.

Integration, rather than elimination, becomes the goal.

This means recognising when a part is active, listening to what it is trying to communicate, and responding with care rather than criticism. It means bringing your present awareness—your adult self—into moments that were once driven entirely by past experience.

As this process unfolds, something begins to settle. The part that is always ready to fight softens slightly. The part that wants to run begins to slow. The part that freezes starts to feel, gradually and safely. The part that has been trying to please learns that it does not have to abandon itself to stay connected.

And as these shifts occur, something new begins to emerge.

A sense of coherence. A sense of wholeness that does not come from being perfect, but from being integrated.

You are not meant to return to who you were before trauma. That version of you existed in a different set of conditions. Healing is not about going back. It is about moving forward with awareness.

It is about becoming someone who understands their own patterns, who can hold complexity without becoming overwhelmed by it, who can feel without being consumed, and who can respond rather than react.

Someone who is whole—not because every part has disappeared, but because every part has been acknowledged.

There is nothing inside you that needs to be rejected. There is nothing that makes you too much, too complicated, or beyond repair. What you are experiencing is not brokenness.

It is layering.

And every layer has a story worth hearing.

CHAPTER 8

Reclaiming Power

Boundaries, Voice, and Choice in Recovery

For a long time, I didn't think of myself as someone who had lost power. That language didn't fit. From the outside, my life still looked intact. I was functioning, making decisions, showing up in the world in ways that would have been read as capable, even strong. But there was something underneath that I couldn't name at the time—a subtle hesitation that showed up in moments where I would pause, second-guess, or adjust before I even realised I was doing it.

It didn't happen all at once. There was no clear moment where I could say something had been taken. It revealed itself slowly, in the way small decisions began to feel heavier than they should have. I would check in with myself and find no clear answer, only a sense of what might keep things calm, what might avoid tension, what might not create a reaction. Over time, that became the reference point. Not what I needed, not what I felt, but what would keep things manageable.

I didn't recognise this as a loss of power. I thought it was awareness. I thought it was maturity. I thought it was knowing how to navigate situations without escalating them.

It took much longer to see that something else had happened beneath that. I had stopped trusting myself. Not in a way that was obvious or dramatic, but in a quiet, consistent way that shaped how I moved through everything.

There was a growing gap between what I felt and what I allowed myself to act on. I would notice discomfort and immediately begin explaining it away. I would soften it, rationalise it, or reinterpret it into something more acceptable. It became automatic. That internal negotiation between instinct and permission. And over time, I moved further away from myself without fully realising it.

The first time I tried to do something different, it wasn't significant. There was no confrontation, no clear turning point. It was a small decision to say no to something that didn't feel right. Logically, it made sense. But my body reacted as though I had done something wrong. There was an immediate tightening in my chest, a rush of doubt, and a strong pull to correct it—to soften what I had said, to explain it, to make it easier for the other person to accept.

That reaction didn't belong to the present moment. It came from somewhere older. At some point, saying no had not been neutral. It had led to conflict, withdrawal, or escalation. My system had learned that, and it responded accordingly.

That was when I began to understand that reclaiming power wouldn't feel powerful, at least not at first. It would feel unfamiliar, and unfamiliar often felt unsafe.

There was a period where nothing dramatic changed externally, but everything began to shift internally. I started paying attention in a different way. Not to what was happening around me, but to what was happening within me. I noticed the moment before I responded, the hesitation before I agreed to something, the flicker of discomfort I used to override without thinking. I didn't always act on it, but I noticed it. And once I noticed it, I couldn't go back to not seeing it.

I had always thought of boundaries as something structured and explicit, something that needed to be explained and understood. What I began to realise was that they were much simpler than that. A boundary was not something I delivered. It was something I chose. Sometimes that choice was expressed in words, and sometimes it wasn't. Sometimes it was simply deciding not to engage, not to continue, not to override what I was feeling in order to maintain a sense of ease.

At first, that felt incomplete, as though I hadn't done enough to justify the decision. But over time, I understood that I didn't need to justify it. I didn't need to make it make sense to anyone else. What mattered was that it made sense to me. That I was no longer automatically moving away from myself.

My voice returned in a similar way. Not suddenly, and not with confidence, but in small, uneven moments where I chose to say something instead of staying silent. There were times where my words felt uncertain, where I questioned them immediately after speaking. There were moments where I wanted to take them back or reshape them into something safer. But each time I allowed them to stand, something shifted internally. I began to experience myself as someone who could exist within my own perspective, rather than constantly adjusting it to fit someone else's expectations.

The most significant shift came in something much simpler than I would have expected. It came in the experience of choice. I hadn't realised how many of my responses had become automatic, how often I moved through situations without recognising that there were other options available.

Recovery didn't restore choice all at once. It appeared in small moments—the pause before responding, the awareness that I could say yes or no, that I could stay or leave, that I could engage or step back.

At first, those moments were easy to miss. But the more I noticed them, the more they expanded. And with that expansion came a sense of agency that had been absent for a long time. It didn't feel dramatic or empowering in the way I had imagined. It felt steady. Grounded. Real.

It didn't begin in the situations that mattered most. It began in the ordinary ones. Choosing what I wanted instead of what was expected. Taking time before responding. Saying no to something minor and allowing that to be enough. These moments didn't feel significant, but they were building something essential—trust. Not trust in others, but trust in myself.

There were people who didn't respond well to those changes. There were moments where the familiar patterns shifted, where something I said or did disrupted what had previously been predictable. At first, that made me question whether I had done something wrong. Over time, I came to understand it differently. It wasn't a failure. It was evidence that something had changed.

There was a belief underlying much of this that I hadn't examined before. The belief that I should not be too much. Not too visible, not too expressive, not too demanding. It had shaped how I showed up in ways I hadn't consciously recognised. Recovery didn't remove that belief immediately, but it created enough distance for me to begin questioning it. To consider the possibility that I didn't need to reduce myself in order to be accepted.

Reclaiming power didn't feel like becoming stronger. It felt like becoming more honest, and getting comfortable with being completely honest. It felt like allowing what I knew internally to exist without immediately reshaping it into something more acceptable. It wasn't a single moment of change, but a series of small decisions made over time. Decisions to stay with myself, to acknowledge what I felt, and to act in alignment with it, even when it felt uncomfortable.

None of those moments would have appeared significant from the outside. But over time, they altered something fundamental in the way I experienced myself.

Power, as I understand it now, is not about control or dominance.

It's honesty.
It's truth telling.
It does not require force.
It is not something that needs to be asserted over others.
It is something quieter and more stable than that. It exists in the ability to remain connected to yourself, to recognise

what is true for you, and to act from that place without abandoning it. To live in your truth.

It returns gradually, in the moments where you stop overriding yourself. Not all at once, but in pieces. And once it begins to return, it does so in a way that is steady, grounded, and entirely your own.

CHAPTER 9

The Journey of Self-Compassion

Learning to Love the Survivor Within

For a long time, compassion felt like something I understood well. I could sit with other people's pain without needing to fix it. I could hear their stories and recognise the layers underneath what had happened to them. I could see context, pressure, fear, and the limits of what they knew at the time. I could offer patience without effort, and care without question. It came naturally, almost instinctively. But when I turned that same attention toward myself, something shifted. The tone changed in a way I didn't immediately recognise.

When I thought about my own story, the space that existed for others disappeared. In its place was something sharper, more precise, less forgiving. I didn't notice it as a separate voice. It didn't feel like something external or intrusive. It felt like truth. It showed up in the way I replayed things, in the questions I asked myself after something had already happened, in the quiet certainty that I should have known better. I would go back over moments, looking for the point where I missed something, where I could have made a different decision, where I could have prevented what came next. There was a logic to it that made it hard to challenge. If I could just understand where I went wrong, then I could make sure it didn't happen again.

That way of thinking didn't feel cruel. It felt responsible. It felt like I was holding myself to a standard that mattered. But underneath it, there was something else I wasn't acknowledging. Every time I approached myself this way, I was narrowing the story. Reducing everything to a single question of fault, of failure, of personal error. It left no room for context, no room for what I was navigating at the time, no room for the fact that I was responding to something I didn't yet fully understand.

It took time before I could see where that voice had come from. It wasn't something that had appeared out of nowhere. It had been shaped gradually, through experiences where my feelings weren't always met with understanding, where responsibility was blurred, where I learned to look inward for the cause of things that were happening around me.

Over time, those patterns settled in. They became part of how I interpreted myself. The voice that questioned, corrected, and tightened around every perceived mistake had developed for a reason. It was trying to keep things controlled, to make sense of uncertainty, to prevent something from going wrong again. It was, in its own way, protective.

Understanding that didn't make it disappear, but it changed how I related to it. Instead of taking it at face value, I started noticing when it showed up. I began to recognise the situations that triggered it, the moments where something felt uncertain or uncomfortable, and how quickly that discomfort turned into self-criticism. The voice wasn't responding to clarity. It was responding to something underneath it. Most of the time, it was fear, or confusion, or the feeling of not being grounded in what was happening.

The criticism came in quickly, giving shape to something that felt harder to sit with.

There was a point where I began to interrupt that pattern, not by replacing it immediately, but by pausing long enough to notice it. Instead of following it all the way through, I would stop and sit with what was actually there. Not for long, just enough to register it.

That small shift changed something. It created a gap between the feeling and the response. In that gap, other questions started to emerge.

Not what I had done wrong, but what had been happening for me at the time.

Not what I should have known, but what I actually knew in that moment.

Those questions didn't remove the discomfort, but they allowed me to hold it differently.

The change wasn't immediate, and it wasn't consistent. There were still moments where I slipped back into the same pattern, where I could feel the pull to analyse, to correct, to reduce everything down to something I could control. But I didn't stay there in the same way. I could see it happening, and that made it possible to step back, even slightly. That distance mattered. It meant I wasn't fully inside it anymore.

For a long time, I had believed that if I could just get everything right, then things would settle. That if I could respond perfectly, understand everything clearly, and avoid repeating the same patterns, I would finally feel okay. That belief sat quietly behind everything I was doing. It kept me striving, measuring, adjusting. Letting go of that didn't happen all at once, but I began to see that it wasn't leading anywhere new. It was keeping me in the same place, just with a different set of expectations.

As that shifted, the way I responded to myself began to change. Not in a way that felt forced or overly positive, but in a way that created more space.

I could acknowledge when something was hard without immediately turning it into a failure. I could recognise that my reactions made sense in the context of what I had been through, even if I wanted to respond differently now. I didn't have to ignore what needed to change, but I didn't have to punish myself in order to change it.

There were still moments where things felt heavy, where I questioned myself, where I felt like I had taken a step backwards. But I didn't turn those moments into something permanent. I could let them be what they were. A response. A reaction. A moment in time. That shift made it possible to keep moving without collapsing into it.

Part of this change came from something outside of me.

From being in spaces where I was met differently than I had been before. Where my experiences were not questioned or minimised, where I didn't have to explain them in order for them to be taken seriously. Where the focus wasn't appointing blame. At first, that felt unfamiliar, but over time it settled in. And gradually, I began to relate to myself in a similar way. Not perfectly, and not all the time, but enough that it began to feel real.

What changed most was not the difficulty of the process, but the way I stayed with myself while I was moving through it. There was less urgency to fix everything immediately, less pressure to understand everything at once. There was more patience, more willingness to let things unfold without forcing them into something they weren't.

It didn't feel like a breakthrough. It felt quieter than that. More like something settling into place over time. And within that, something else began to grow. Not confidence in the way I had once understood it, but a steadiness. A sense that I didn't have to abandon myself in order to move forward.

I began to understand that compassion wasn't something I had to earn. Not through getting it right, not through proving anything, not through becoming someone different. It was something I was allowed to have, even in the middle of not knowing, even in the middle of learning.

And from that place, something became possible that hadn't been before. Not just change, but a different relationship with myself as that change unfolded.

CHAPTER 10

The Body Remembers - Healing Trauma Through Mind and Body

Long after everything has changed on the outside, something inside can still feel the same. Life can look stable. Calm, even. The relationship is over, the environment is different, the immediate danger is no longer there.

And yet, there are moments where the body reacts as though nothing has changed at all. A tightening in the chest that comes without warning. A sudden alertness that doesn't match the situation. A sense of being braced, as though something is about to happen, even when there is no clear reason for it.

For a long time, I didn't understand that. I thought if the situation had ended, then the feeling should end with it. I thought once I was safe, I would feel safe. When that didn't happen, I questioned myself. I wondered why I was still reacting, why something so small could shift my entire state, why calm never seemed to settle fully in my body, even when I could see that everything around me was okay.

It didn't feel logical. It felt like something I should have been able to control.

What I didn't understand then was that my body wasn't responding to what was happening in front of me. It was responding to what it had learned to expect.

The reactions didn't come as thoughts. They came as sensations. A racing heart, a knot in my stomach, a sudden drop in energy, or the opposite—a surge of restlessness that made it impossible to sit still. Sometimes it felt like heat rising through my body, other times like everything inside me had gone quiet and distant. There were moments where I felt like I needed to get away, even when there was nowhere I needed to go. Moments where I shut down without meaning to, as though something had switched off internally.

I didn't have language for it at the time. I just knew that my body wasn't responding in the way I expected it to.

It took time to understand that this wasn't random. There was a system underneath it, something that had been shaped over time through repetition, through exposure, through the constant need to assess what was safe and what wasn't. That system didn't rely on conscious thought. It worked quickly, automatically, scanning for cues, making decisions before I was even aware of them.

Its role was simple. **To keep me safe.**

The problem wasn't that it was doing its job. The problem was that it had learned in an environment where safety was inconsistent, where things could shift quickly, where being alert made sense. So it stayed that way. Even when the environment changed, the pattern didn't immediately update. It continued to respond as though the conditions were the same.

That's why I could know, logically, that I was safe, and still feel unsafe.

The knowing didn't reach the part of me that was reacting.

There were times where my body stayed in a state of activation for longer than I could understand. A constant tension that didn't fully settle. Difficulty sleeping, even when I was exhausted. A sense of being on edge, as though something needed my attention at all times. Other times, it moved in the opposite direction. Everything slowed down. My energy dropped, my thoughts became distant, and it felt like I was moving through things without fully being there.

At first, I saw those responses as problems I needed to fix. Something to control, something to override. I tried to think my way out of them, to reason with them, to remind myself that nothing was wrong. Sometimes that helped briefly, but it didn't last. The reaction would come back, often in a different form, as though it hadn't been addressed at all.

It was frustrating, because I understood what was happening, at least on the surface. I could explain it. I could make sense of it. But my body wasn't responding to that understanding.

That was when I started to realise that understanding alone wasn't enough.

What I was experiencing wasn't just stored in my thoughts. It was held in my body. And my body didn't respond to logic in the same way my mind did. It responded to experience. To what it could feel, not what it could be told.

That shifted the way I approached it.

Instead of trying to control the response, I started paying attention to it. Not in a way that overwhelmed me, but in small moments. Noticing where I felt tension. Noticing my breath. Noticing when my body was braced without me realising it. It wasn't about analysing it. It was about becoming aware of it.

At first, even that felt unfamiliar. My body didn't feel like a place I wanted to be. It felt unpredictable, sometimes overwhelming, sometimes distant. But I didn't force it. I didn't try to change everything at once. I stayed with what I could tolerate, what felt manageable in the moment.

Sometimes that was as simple as noticing my feet on the ground, or the way a chair supported my body. Sometimes it was taking a breath and letting it be slightly slower than the one before it. Nothing dramatic. Nothing that required effort.

But those moments added up.

I began to see that the goal wasn't to control my body into being calm. It was to support it in finding its way back to a state where calm was possible. There was a difference between forcing something and allowing something. One created more tension. The other created space.

That space mattered.

Because the nervous system doesn't respond to words alone. It responds to what it experiences. The environment, the tone of someone's voice, the pace of an interaction, the presence of someone who is steady—these things communicate safety in a way that explanation never can.

There were moments where I could feel the difference. Spaces where I wasn't rushed, where I wasn't expected to be anything other than what I was in that moment. Spaces where I didn't have to explain myself into something more acceptable. At first, those moments felt unfamiliar. But over time, they began to register differently. My body responded to them, even when my mind didn't fully recognise it.

Slowly, those experiences started to accumulate.

And something began to shift.

There were still times where I was triggered, where something in the present connected to something in the past, and my body reacted as though it was happening again. A tone, a look, a situation—something small that carried a familiarity I couldn't always place. The reaction would come quickly, before I had time to think.

But I started to understand that differently too.

It wasn't about what was happening in that moment. It was about what my body was remembering.

That changed the question.

Instead of asking why I was reacting like that, I began to ask what it was connected to. Not always in detail, not always with a clear answer, but enough to recognise that the response made sense in context, even if it didn't match the present.

That understanding didn't stop the reaction from happening, but it changed how I met it.

Instead of fighting it, I stayed with it. Not forcing myself to remain in something overwhelming, but gently increasing my capacity to be present with myself while it moved through. Even for a few seconds longer than I could before.

That mattered more than I expected.

Because each time I did that, something shifted. Not dramatically, but enough. Enough to build a sense that I could stay with myself without needing to escape the moment entirely.

For a long time, my body had felt like something that worked against me. The panic, the shutdown, the sensations that didn't seem to make sense—they felt like something I needed to fix or control.

But that changed.

I began to see that my body wasn't the problem. It had been trying to protect me the entire time.

Even when the responses no longer matched the situation, they had developed for a reason. They had carried me through something that required adaptation, that required awareness, that required survival.

That recognition shifted something fundamental.

Instead of seeing my body as something I needed to override, I started relating to it as something I needed to understand.

Healing didn't come from forcing it into calm. It came from creating enough safety that calm could emerge on its own. It showed up in small moments—a breath that went a little deeper, a muscle that softened without me telling it to, a brief sense of stillness that didn't immediately disappear.

Those moments didn't feel significant on their own.

But they built. And over time, they began to outweigh the constant state of being on edge.

My body still holds my story.

Not just the parts that were difficult, but the parts that endured. The parts that adapted, that stayed, that carried me through when I didn't know how to carry myself.

Healing hasn't been about leaving that behind. It has been about coming back to it. Slowly, patiently, and in a way that allows my body to learn something new.

That it is no longer alone in holding everything.

And that, over time, it can become a place I feel safe to be again.

PART II: FRAMEWORK

CHAPTER 11

The Steps of Survivors Anonymous

Recovery didn't feel unclear because I didn't want to heal. It felt unclear because I didn't know where to begin.

There was too much of everything. Too many layers, too many questions, too many things that felt unfinished. I could see the impact of what had happened to me, but I couldn't see a clear way through it. One day I would feel like I understood something, like I had found a piece of clarity, and the next day it would feel like I was back at the beginning again. Not because I had lost progress, but because everything was connected, and pulling on one thread seemed to bring ten others with it.

That was the part no one had explained.

It wasn't just the weight of what I had been through. It was the lack of structure around how to move through it.

Without that, everything stayed internal. Circular. I would think about things, reflect on them, try to make sense of them, but there was nothing holding it in place. No sequence. No container. No sense of where I was in the process, or what came next. Just an ongoing attempt to untangle something that didn't seem to have a clear starting point or an obvious end.

That's where people get stuck.

Not because they aren't trying, but because they are trying to process something complex without anything to hold it.

And without something to hold it, the mind does what it can. It loops. It revisits. It replays. It searches for answers in places that don't actually move anything forward. It becomes overwhelming, not because healing is impossible, but because it is uncontained.

That's where a framework becomes necessary.

Not as a set of rules. Not as something rigid or prescriptive. But as something that creates shape around the process. Something that allows movement without requiring everything to be understood at once. Something that gives you a place to stand while you are working through things that feel unsteady.

What I needed wasn't more insight.

I needed a way through.

The original twelve steps were designed for addiction recovery, and they work because they give people that structure. They take something that feels chaotic and overwhelming and break it down into something that can be approached one step at a time. They create movement where there would otherwise be paralysis.

But trauma doesn't move in the same way.

It isn't just about behaviour. It isn't just about patterns you can see clearly and decide to change. It lives in the body, in the nervous system, in the way responses have been shaped over time without conscious awareness. It involves memory, identity, safety, connection, and meaning, all layered together in ways that don't separate neatly.

So while the structure of the steps is powerful, the lens they are viewed through matters.

Survivors Anonymous comes from that understanding.

Not from the idea that you are the problem that needs to be fixed, but from the recognition that you adapted to something that required you to survive. That your responses made sense in context. That what you are carrying is not just behaviour, but experience that has not yet been fully processed or integrated.

The framework doesn't start with blame.

It starts with understanding.

What the steps offer is not a solution in the way people often look for one. They don't remove what has happened, and they don't bypass the complexity of it. What they do is create a pathway.

Not a straight line, but a direction.

They allow you to approach things gradually, instead of trying to hold everything at once. They give you somewhere to begin, and somewhere to return to when things feel unclear again. They create a rhythm to the process, something that moves you forward without forcing you to rush.

Without that, it is easy to stay in reflection without movement.

With it, reflection becomes part of something that leads somewhere.

The steps themselves are simple in how they are written, but not in what they ask of you. They begin with recognition, with the willingness to look at the impact of what has happened without immediately turning away from it. They move into the possibility of healing, into the idea that something different can exist, even if you don't fully believe it yet. They ask you to begin loosening the need to control everything, not all at once, but enough to allow something new to emerge.

From there, the work deepens. It becomes about looking at your experiences with honesty, but without the layer of shame that so often sits on top of them. It becomes about allowing yourself to be seen, not by everyone, but in spaces that are safe enough to hold that. It involves recognising the patterns and strategies that once protected you, and beginning to question whether they are still serving you now.

There is a point where the focus shifts outward as well as inward. Where you begin to see the impact that trauma has had on your relationships, not as a source of guilt, but as something that can be understood and, where possible, repaired. Not perfectly, and not at the cost of your own safety, but in a way that aligns with who you are becoming.

The later steps move into something quieter, but just as important. Ongoing awareness. A deeper connection to yourself. A sense of meaning that is not defined by what has happened to you, but by how you choose to live with it. And eventually, a recognition that healing doesn't end with you. That what you have learned, what you have lived through, can become something that supports others.

There is no point in this process where you are expected to get it right.

That's not how this works.

You may move through the steps in order, or you may find yourself returning to the same place more than once. You may sit with something for longer than you expected, or move through something more quickly than you thought you would. None of that means you are doing it wrong.

It means you are doing it in a way that is real.

The most important part of this, the part that sits underneath everything else, is safety.

Not in an abstract sense, but in a practical one.

You choose what you engage with. You choose what you share, when you share it, and how far you go. There is no requirement to revisit something before you are ready, no expectation that you move at a pace that doesn't feel manageable. You are allowed to pause, to step back, to take time.

Healing that is forced doesn't hold. Healing that is supported does.

There will be days where it feels like movement, where something makes sense in a way it didn't before. There will also be days where it feels like you have gone backwards, where old patterns show up, where things feel just as tangled as they did at the beginning.

That doesn't mean nothing is changing.

It means the process is working at a depth that isn't always visible.

Recovery isn't linear. It doesn't move in a straight line from beginning to end. It layers. It revisits. It unfolds over time. And all of it counts.

This is not something that was ever meant to be done alone.

You can move through parts of it by yourself, but healing deepens in places where you are not the only one holding it. In spaces where you don't have to explain everything for it to be understood. Where you are not compared, not measured, not reduced to what has happened to you.

That is what Survivors Anonymous is meant to be.

Not just a framework. A place where that framework can be lived.

You don't need to have everything figured out before you begin. You don't need to feel ready in a complete or certain way. You don't even need to fully believe that it will work.

You just need a willingness to take one step.

Not all of them.

Just one.

Recovery doesn't happen all at once. It doesn't arrive as a finished version of yourself.

It happens gradually, in the decisions you make, in the way you begin to understand what you have been through, in the way you learn to stay with yourself instead of moving away.

The steps are not a destination.

They are a way of walking through something that would otherwise feel impossible to navigate.

And you are allowed to move through them in your own time.

CHAPTER 12

How It Works

Rarely have we seen someone remain unchanged when they have been willing to walk this path with honesty, courage, and support. This is not because recovery is easy. It is because something begins to shift when we stop running from ourselves, and instead begin to understand—gently, truthfully—what has shaped us.

This is not a program built on perfection. It is a process built on willingness. Those who struggle most are not those who are incapable. They are often those who have been hurt so deeply that turning inward feels unsafe. For many of us, our survival depended on not seeing clearly. On minimising what happened. On disconnecting from how we felt. On adapting in ways that helped us endure. So if you find this difficult—if parts of you resist this work—you are not failing.

You are responding exactly as your nervous system was shaped to respond. There is nothing wrong with you for surviving the way you did. What we offer here is not a set of rules. It is a pathway. Our stories are not here to compare pain or measure strength. They are here to show, in a general way: what we lived through, how we survived and what became possible when we began to understand ourselves differently.

If you are reading this and something in you is saying, *"I don't want to live like this anymore"* then you are ready. You may not feel ready. You may feel unsure, overwhelmed, resistant, or even numb. That's okay. Most of us did too. We tried to find easier ways. Ways that didn't require us to feel. Ways that allowed us to keep the same patterns that once kept us safe. But eventually, we saw something clearly: what protected us once… was now keeping us stuck. And that is where this work begins.

Domestic and family violence does not just impact your life. It shapes your body, your thinking, your relationships, and your sense of self. You may have: doubted your own reality, stayed when you wanted to leave, returned when you knew it wasn't safe, lost connection with who you were, or adapted in ways that no longer make sense now. And somewhere along the way, you may have started asking: *"Why did I do that?" "What's wrong with me?"*

This chapter invites a different question:

"What happened to me—and how did I survive it?"

Because everything begins to change when we shift from blame to understanding. In Survivors Anonymous, we recognise that: your patterns are not moral failings - They are trauma responses, survival strategies, and nervous system adaptations. Your body learned when to speak, when to stay silent, when to appease, when to freeze, when to disconnect. Not because you were weak. But because those responses helped you survive. And now, those same responses may be showing up in ways that keep you stuck, keep you small - keep you unsafe.

This is not your fault. But it is something you can begin to change. Not through force. Not through shame. But through awareness, support, and safety. At some point, many of us reached a place where we realised we could not think our way out of this. We had insight. We had understanding. We had moments of clarity. But we still repeated patterns, felt overwhelmed, and struggled to change.

Because this is not just about thinking.

It is about **a nervous system shaped by survival**

And healing that requires something different.

It requires safety, connection, honesty, support.. And most importantly **it requires that we stop doing this alone.**

These steps are not rules. They are not a test you must pass. They are **a guide toward reconnection—with yourself, your life, and your sense of safety.** You do not have to do them perfectly. You only have to be willing. Here are the steps we took, which are suggested as the program of recovery:

1 - We acknowledge that what we have been through has impacted us deeply, and that parts of our lives feel out of our control.

2 - We begin to believe that healing is possible, and that support—within and beyond ourselves—can help restore clarity and stability.

3 - We choose to stop doing this alone, and begin to trust something outside of survival mode.

4 - We gently begin to look at our experiences, our patterns, and our responses with honesty and compassion.

5 - We share our truth—with ourselves and with someone safe—breaking the silence that kept us isolated.

6 - We become willing to release the patterns that no longer serve us, even if they once kept us safe.

7 - We allow ourselves to receive support in letting go, understanding that change happens through safety, not force.

8 - We reflect on harm in our lives—what was done to us, and where our survival responses may have impacted others.

9 - Where it is safe, we begin to repair—without placing ourselves at risk, and without taking responsibility for harm that was not ours.

10 - We continue to notice our patterns and gently return to awareness when we drift into old ways.

11 - We develop a relationship with stillness, reflection, or something greater than ourselves—whatever that means to us.

12 - As we heal, we begin to support others and live these principles in our everyday lives.

Many of us looked at these steps and thought *"This is too much." "I can't do this." "This is going to be too triggering..."*

And the truth is you don't have to do it all at once. You don't even have to believe all of it yet. You just have to be open enough to consider, and stay open enough to begin. We are not aiming for perfection. We are not trying to erase the past. We know that never goes away.

Instead we are moving toward **progress, awareness, and safety.** You are not responsible for the harm that was done to you. But as you heal, you may begin to notice patterns in your relationships, ways you respond to fear, and ways you protect yourself.

This is not about blame.

It is about **giving yourself the power to choose differently. This** work is not about becoming someone new. It is about: **returning to yourself—before survival took over.**

To the parts of you that were clear, grounded, connected, alive and joyful. Those parts are still there. They have just been protected. You are not broken. You adapted. And now, step by step, with support and understanding, **you are learning how to live beyond survival.**

CHAPTER 13

Step One

Admitting the Impact of Trauma

"We acknowledged the impact that trauma has had on our lives, and recognised that survival responses once kept us safe, but may no longer serve us".

Step One begins with a shift that is simple in its wording, but often difficult in practice. It asks you to acknowledge the impact that trauma has had on your life, and to recognise that the ways you adapted to survive may no longer serve you in the present. At its core, this step is about telling the truth, but not in the way many people initially expect.

This is not about assigning blame or dissecting every detail of what happened. It is not about proving the severity of your experience or measuring it against anyone else's. The purpose of this step is not to determine whether something was "bad enough." It is to recognise, with honesty, that it had an impact. That it changed something in you. That it shaped how you think, how you feel, how you respond, and how you move through the world.

For many survivors, this is unfamiliar territory. There is often a long history of minimising what happened, explaining it away, or focusing on other people's experiences instead of your own. You may have learned to take responsibility for things that were never yours to carry, or to reduce your own experience to make it more acceptable or easier to hold. Because of this, the question that tends to come up is not "What did this do to me?" but "Was it really that bad?"

Step One gently redirects that question. It moves away from evaluating the event and toward understanding its impact. The focus is not on whether it meets a certain threshold, but on how it has affected you. This distinction matters, because trauma is not defined solely by what happened. It is defined by what happened inside you as a result.

The impact of trauma does not always present in obvious or dramatic ways. It often shows up in patterns that develop over time, in the way your body responds to stress, in the way you relate to others, and in the way you interpret yourself.

You might notice a constant sense of alertness, difficulty trusting people even when they have given you no reason not to, or a tendency to prioritise other people's needs at the expense of your own. You may find yourself overwhelmed by emotions at times, or disconnected from them entirely. You may recognise recurring patterns in relationships, a reliance on coping behaviours that once provided relief, or a critical inner voice that is difficult to quiet.

None of these responses are random. They are connected, even if they do not initially appear to be. They are part of the story your body and mind have been carrying, often without your conscious awareness. Step One creates the space to begin seeing those connections, not as evidence that something is wrong with you, but as evidence that something has happened to you.

One of the most common barriers in this step is comparison. It can be difficult to acknowledge your own experience when there is a tendency to measure it against others. You may find yourself thinking that other people have had it worse, or that you should have been able to handle it differently, or that enough time has passed that it should no longer affect you. These thoughts can keep you from fully engaging with the process, because they shift the focus away from your own experience and back into evaluation.

Step One invites you to let go of that comparison. Trauma does not operate on a fixed scale. Two people can go through the same situation and be affected in entirely different ways, and both experiences are valid. What matters is not how it compares, but how it has shaped you. If something has had a lasting impact on your life, it deserves to be acknowledged.

Alongside this recognition comes something equally important. The understanding that the ways you responded made sense at the time. The patterns, behaviours, and survival strategies you developed were not arbitrary. They were adaptations to circumstances that required you to find a way through. They helped you stay safe, maintain connection where possible, and cope with situations that may have felt overwhelming or inescapable.

This does not mean those responses are still helpful now. In many cases, the very things that once supported your survival can begin to limit you. You may find yourself reacting to situations that are no longer dangerous, struggling to trust people who are safe, or avoiding opportunities that could support your growth. These patterns are not signs of failure. They are the result of a system that has learned to prioritise safety based on past experience.

The purpose of Step One is not to eliminate those responses, but to bring awareness to them. To recognise where they came from, how they developed, and how they continue to influence your life. This awareness creates the foundation for everything that follows, because it shifts the way you understand yourself.

Instead of asking what is wrong with you, you begin to ask what has happened to you, and how it has shaped the way you respond. This shift may seem subtle, but it changes the entire framework. It moves you out of self-blame and into understanding. It allows you to see your patterns in context, rather than as isolated problems that need to be fixed.

Telling the truth about impact can feel confronting. There may be emotions that surface as you begin to see things more clearly. Grief, anger, confusion, and even relief can all be part of this process. These responses are not a sign that you are doing something wrong. They are a sign that you are allowing yourself to see what has been there, often for a long time.

Step One does not require you to become overwhelmed by the past. It simply asks you to acknowledge it. To bring it out of the background and into awareness, where it can begin to be understood rather than unconsciously repeated.

You do not need to have a complete or detailed understanding in order to begin. It can start with a simple recognition that what you went through has affected you, that there are patterns in your life connected to your past, and that you have been carrying more than you may have realised. That level of honesty is enough to open the door.

There is also something important to recognise here that can easily be overlooked. **You made it through.** Whatever you experienced, and however it has affected you, **you are still here**. Step One is not only about acknowledging pain. It is also about ***recognising resilience***, even if you have never used that word to describe yourself.

This step marks the beginning of a different relationship with your experience. One that is not built on minimising, denying, or explaining things away, but on recognising them as they are. It creates the foundation for healing, not by forcing change, but by allowing clarity.

From that place, something becomes possible that was not accessible before. Not because everything is resolved, but because it is no longer hidden.

And that is where the process begins.

CHAPTER 14

Step Two

Believing in Something Greater

"We came to believe that there is something greater than our current state that can restore us to wholeness."

Step Two has a clear purpose, even if it doesn't feel clear at first. It is about coming to believe that there is something greater than the state you are currently in that can restore you to your whole self. Not a perfect version of yourself, not a fixed or finished version, but a version of you that is no longer defined by survival alone.

For many people, that idea does not land easily. Belief is not something that feels available. After trauma, it is common for trust to narrow, sometimes to the point where it only includes what can be controlled. Experiences that involved harm, unpredictability, or betrayal can reshape the way you see the world, and over time, it can feel safer not to rely on anything outside of yourself. In that space, the idea that something greater could support you, guide you, or restore you can feel distant or unrealistic.

This step does not ask you to force belief into existence. It does not require certainty, and it does not expect you to arrive at a fully formed understanding. The purpose is not to declare belief, but to come to it. That distinction matters, because belief that is forced does not hold. Belief that develops gradually, through experience and recognition, is something that can be sustained.

Coming to believe is a process.

It begins with a shift in position. Instead of holding tightly to what you already know, even if what you know is shaped by pain, you begin to allow the possibility that there may be something beyond it. Not as a conclusion, but as an opening. A recognition that your current experience, as real and as valid as it is, may not be the full picture of what is possible for you.

For some people, this begins with noticing others. Seeing people who have lived through similar experiences and recognising that something in them has changed. Not in a way that erases what they have been through, but in a way that shows movement, stability, or a sense of self that is no longer defined by what happened to them. That observation matters, because it introduces evidence. Not theoretical evidence, but lived evidence that change is possible.

For others, it begins in smaller moments. A sense of relief that appears briefly and then fades. A moment of connection that feels different from what has been experienced before. A feeling of being understood without having to explain everything. These moments may not feel significant at first, but they are part of how belief starts to form. They interrupt the assumption that everything will always feel the same.

Belief often begins before it is fully recognised.

It can show up as a quiet thought that things could be different, even if that thought is quickly dismissed. It can appear as curiosity, or as a willingness to keep engaging with something that you do not yet fully trust. It can exist as a small part of you that has not given up, even when everything else feels uncertain.

This is where the process of coming to believe takes shape.

It is not about finding the right definition of something greater. It is about recognising that there is something beyond your current state that is capable of supporting change. For some, that is found in spirituality. For others, it is found in connection with other people, in shared experience, or in a sense of meaning that develops over time. It may be found in the consistency of a safe relationship, in the structure of a recovery space, or in the growing awareness that you are not as alone as you once believed.

What matters is not the label you give it, but the role it begins to play.

The purpose of this step is to shift you out of isolation and into relationship with something that is not limited by your past experiences. That shift is what allows restoration to become possible. Not because something external fixes you, but because you are no longer relying solely on the patterns that were shaped in survival.

There is also an important recognition within this step that restoration does not come from force. It does not come from trying harder, thinking differently, or controlling your responses more effectively. It comes from allowing something new to enter the process. Something that is not driven by fear, by hypervigilance, or by the need to stay ahead of potential harm.

Coming to believe is what makes that possible. It creates enough space for a different experience to take hold.

That space may feel unfamiliar at first. You may notice resistance, doubt, or a tendency to pull back into what feels known and predictable. That is part of the process. Belief does not replace those responses immediately. It develops alongside them, gradually becoming more accessible as new experiences begin to reinforce it.

Over time, what was once only a possibility can begin to feel more real.

Not because you have convinced yourself of it, but because you have experienced moments that support it. Moments where you feel less alone, where you respond differently than you would have before, where something in you settles in a way that it previously could not. These moments are not separate from the process. They are the process.

This is how belief forms.

Not as a single decision, but as a series of experiences that begin to shift what you understand to be true.

Step Two does not require you to arrive at certainty. It asks you to remain open long enough for belief to begin to take shape. To recognise that your current way of being is not the only way available to you, and that something beyond it has the capacity to support your return to yourself.

The restoration that this step speaks to is not about becoming someone new. It is about reconnecting with parts of yourself that were shaped, protected, or hidden in order to survive. It is about allowing those parts to exist in a different context, one where they are no longer required to carry everything on their own.

Coming to believe is what makes that reconnection possible.

It is the point where something begins to shift, even if that shift is small.

And that is enough to continue.

CHAPTER 15

Step Three

Turning Toward Something Greater

"We made a decision to begin releasing control, and to turn our will and care toward something greater than our survival-driven thinking."

Step Three is where the process becomes more deliberate. It is the point where you move from considering the possibility of something greater into making a decision to relate to it. Not perfectly, not with certainty, but with intention. The purpose of this step is to begin releasing the need to control everything, and to turn your will and your care over to something greater than your own survival-driven thinking. Not in a way that removes your agency, but in a way that allows you to stop carrying what was never yours to hold alone.

For many survivors, control is not something that feels optional. It developed for a reason. When your environment has been unpredictable, unsafe, or shaped by someone else's power, control becomes a way to create stability. You learn to anticipate what others need, to read situations before they escalate, to adjust yourself in ways that reduce risk. You become aware of everything, because at some point, that awareness mattered. It kept you safer than not paying attention.

Over time, that pattern becomes automatic. It no longer feels like something you are doing. It feels like who you are. The problem is not that it exists. The problem is that it continues long after the conditions that required it have changed. What once protected you begins to exhaust you. You may find yourself thinking ahead constantly, struggling to relax, feeling responsible for things that are outside of your control, or unable to trust that anything will hold together without your effort.

There is often a quiet belief underneath all of this that if you let go, something will go wrong. That if you stop managing everything, things will fall apart. And for many people, that belief is not imagined. At some point, it was true.

Step Three does not ignore that history. It does not ask you to suddenly stop controlling everything or to trust blindly. What it asks is more measured. It asks you to begin noticing what you are holding, and to question whether it is actually yours to carry. It invites you to loosen your grip, gradually, in ways that feel safe enough, rather than forcing a release that your system is not ready for.

This is also the step where the idea of God, or something greater, often becomes complicated. Not because the concept itself is necessarily difficult, but because many people have been given a version of it that was **shaped by control**. For some, God was presented as something to fear, something that judged, punished, or demanded obedience. For others, spirituality was intertwined with authority, used to reinforce power rather than support connection. In those contexts, the idea of turning anything over to God can feel like stepping back into something unsafe.

It is important to recognise that what you were taught is not the same as what is available to you now. The understanding of God that may have been given to you, especially if it was delivered through control, is not the only understanding that exists. In this process, you are not being asked to accept someone else's definition. You are being invited to explore your own.

God, in the context of recovery, does not need to resemble the version you may have been conditioned to accept. It does not need to be rigid, authoritarian, or external in a way that removes your autonomy. It can be understood as something that supports connection rather than control, something that holds space rather than imposes rules, something that exists beyond the limitations of fear-based thinking.

For some people, this will feel spiritual. For others, it may feel more grounded in connection, in the collective strength of others, in the process itself, or in a sense of meaning that develops over time. What matters is not the label, but the function. It needs to be something that exists outside of the patterns that were shaped in survival, something that is not driven by fear, hypervigilance, or the need to manage every outcome.

Turning your will and your care over does not mean giving up your ability to choose. It does not mean becoming passive or ignoring your instincts. It means recognising the limits of what control can achieve, and allowing something else to support you where control no longer serves you. It is the difference between carrying everything alone and allowing yourself to be held within something larger than your own effort.

This process does not happen all at once. It begins in small moments. Moments where you notice that you are trying to control something that is not within your power, and you pause. Moments where you allow uncertainty to exist without immediately trying to resolve it. Moments where you recognise that you do not have to anticipate every outcome in order to be safe.

There may be resistance here. Letting go of control can feel unfamiliar, and at times unsafe. Your body may respond with tension, with anxiety, with the urge to pull everything back into something you can manage. That response is not a sign that you are doing something wrong. It is a reflection of how necessary control once was. This step is not about overriding that response. It is about working with it, gradually, with awareness.

As you move through this process, clarity begins to emerge around what is yours to hold and what is not. Your choices, your boundaries, your responses, and the way you care for yourself remain yours. Other people's behaviour, their emotions, and the outcomes of situations do not. When those lines become clearer, the need to control everything begins to soften, because you are no longer trying to manage what was never within your control to begin with.

The decision in Step Three is also not about reaching a state of complete surrender. It is about *choosing to begin.* Choosing to loosen your hold on what is exhausting you. Choosing to trust, even in a small way, that you do not have to navigate everything alone. Choosing to allow something greater, however you understand it, to be part of the process.

This decision may feel subtle, but it creates space. Space for something different to emerge. Space for support, for connection, for a way of moving through life that is not defined by constant effort and control.

What you are learning in this step is not how to give up your strength, but how to use it differently. Not in holding everything together, but in allowing yourself to be supported in ways that were not previously available to you.

Control once helped you survive. It created structure where there was chaos and predictability where there was none. But you are not in that same place anymore. And you do not have to carry everything the way you once did.

Step Three is where you begin to put some of that weight down. Not all at once, and not without awareness, but enough to experience something new. A sense that you are not alone in holding your life together. A sense that there is something beyond your own effort that you can begin to trust, even if that trust is still forming.

And from that place, something else becomes possible. Not certainty, but a different kind of steadiness. One that does not come from control, but from connection.

And so now the God question...

In the preceding chapters, we have spoken about trauma, survival, and the ways we learned to cope. We hope we have made clear the distinction between surviving and living.

If, when you truly want to feel safe, you cannot settle your body… If, when you try to change, you find yourself repeating the same patterns…If your reactions seem to take over, even when you know better… then you may be living in a system shaped by trauma.

If that is the case, you may be experiencing something that cannot be resolved by willpower alone. To someone who does not believe in anything beyond themselves — or who has been hurt by systems that claimed to offer help — the idea of healing through something "greater" can feel impossible. And yet, continuing as you are often feels just as impossible.

To remain stuck in cycles of fear, disconnection, or survival…or to consider opening to something unknown… These are not easy choices. But it is not as difficult as it may seem.

Many of us came here questioning everything. Some of us rejected anything that sounded like "spirituality." Others had seen belief used as a weapon — something that harmed rather than healed. Some of us simply stopped believing in anything at all. Still, we reached a point where we had to face a simple truth:

What we had been doing was not working. We had tried to think our way out. We had tried to control our way out. We had tried to become "better," "stronger," or "different." But something was missing. If understanding, insight, or effort were enough, many of us would have healed long ago.

We wanted to change. We tried to change. We promised ourselves we would change. But when the moment came —

when the body activated, when the memory surfaced, when the trigger hit — the power to choose felt absent.

It wasn't that we didn't care. It was that we couldn't access what we needed when it mattered most.

This is not a failure of character. It is a lack of power.

We came to understand that we needed access to something beyond our conditioned responses. Something steadier than fear. Something more grounded than survival. Something that could hold us when we could not hold ourselves. You may call this safety, truth, connection, the body, the nervous system, a higher power, nature, the universe, or something sacred.

Or you may not have a name for it at all. That's okay. This is not about adopting someone else's belief. It is about discovering what *feels real* to you.

Many of us resisted this step. We associated "belief" with weakness. We distrusted anything we could not control. We rejected systems that had failed us. Some of us were deeply sceptical. Others were quietly curious. At times, we questioned everything: How could anything greater exist in a world that allowed harm? Why would we trust something we could not see? What if all of this was meaningless? And yet, even in the midst of doubt, many of us had moments. A sense of awe. A feeling of connection. A brief experience of peace. These moments were often fleeting — but they were real.

We found that we did not need certainty to begin. We did not need to define anything perfectly. We did not need to believe in a specific concept. We only needed to become willing to consider:

Is it possible that there is something beyond the patterns I've been trapped in?

That question alone was enough. From there, something began to shift. Not all at once. Not perfectly. But noticeably. We began to experience small changes like a moment of pause, a different choice, or a sense of direction. This was the beginning of accessing a new kind of power.

Relief came when we realised we do not have to accept anyone else's version of healing, spirituality, or truth. Your understanding — however incomplete — is enough. Your starting point is enough. Growth does not come from certainty. It comes from willingness.

We found that we needed to ask only one simple question:

Am I willing to believe that something beyond my current patterns could help me heal?

If the answer is yes — even slightly — then something has already begun. That willingness becomes the foundation. From it, a new structure can be built - one grounded in safety, guided by truth, and shaped by your own experience

Many of us believed we had to do everything alone. We relied on control, intellect, or independence. We told ourselves that if we just tried harder, we could fix it. But for many of us, that belief became part of the problem. Not because we were incapable… but because we were trying to heal in isolation.

We began to see that connection matters, support matters, something beyond us matters. Not as weakness — but as a different kind of strength.

We often thought we had no faith. But when we looked closely, we realised we trusted our thoughts, we believed in our coping strategies, and we relied on familiar patterns. In truth, we had been living by faith all along — just not always in things that supported us. Now, we are invited to place that faith somewhere else.

Across many different stories, backgrounds, and experiences, one thing became clear: When people opened themselves — even slightly — to something beyond their old patterns, change became possible. Not always dramatic. Not always immediate. But real. People began to feel more grounded, more connected, and more capable of choice than they had ever felt before. They found moments of peace where there had only been chaos. They discovered that healing was not something they had to force — but something they could begin to allow.

We are not here to tell you what to believe. We are here to offer you a possibility That healing may require more than effort alone. That support may exist beyond what you've known. That you do not have to do this entirely on your own. If you are willing to explore that — in your own way, at your own pace — you may find that something begins to shift. And when you begin to move toward it… it will begin to meet you.

CHAPTER 16

Step Four

A Compassionate Inventory

"We explored our experiences, patterns, and beliefs with honesty and compassion, without shame or self-blame."

Step Four is where the work becomes more direct. It is the point where you begin to look at your life with a level of honesty that may not have felt possible before. The purpose of this step is not to expose what is wrong with you, but to understand what has shaped you. It is an invitation to take a full inventory of your experiences, your patterns, your beliefs, and your responses, and to do so through a trauma-informed lens that holds context, not judgment.

For many people, the idea of an inventory immediately brings discomfort. It can sound like scrutiny, like being asked to examine everything under a harsh light. There is often an assumption that this step is about uncovering faults, exposing mistakes, or confronting parts of yourself that feel difficult to face. That is not the purpose here. This is not an exercise in self-criticism. It is an exercise in clarity.

Up until this point, much of your story may have been shaped by survival. You responded in ways that made sense at the time, often without the space or safety to reflect on why. You adapted quickly, sometimes automatically, and those adaptations became part of how you moved through the world. Over time, they can begin to feel like who you are, rather than what you learned to do. Step Four creates the space to look again, but from where you are now, with more awareness and more language than you had before.

This is where the process becomes an excavation.

Not in a way that forces everything to the surface at once, but in a way that allows you to begin uncovering what has been sitting underneath your day-to-day experience. The patterns you repeat, the beliefs you carry, the ways you respond in relationships, the reactions that seem to come out of nowhere. None of these exist in isolation. They are connected, even if they have never been fully named.

As you begin to explore them, you may notice how consistently certain patterns appear. Ways of relating that feel familiar, even when they are not safe. A tendency to overextend yourself, to avoid conflict, to stay quiet when something matters, or to question your own perception when something feels off. You may recognise the way you respond emotionally, either becoming overwhelmed or shutting down entirely. You may see how these responses have followed you across different areas of your life.

The purpose of this step is not to judge those patterns, but to understand where they came from.

Beneath the patterns, there are often beliefs that formed over time. Beliefs about who you are, what you deserve, and how the world works. These beliefs are rarely chosen consciously. They develop gradually, shaped by repeated experiences, by what was reinforced, what was dismissed, and what was required in order to stay safe or connected. Over time, they begin to feel like facts, even when they are not.

This is where the work deepens, because it is not just about seeing what you do, but understanding why you do it. Why certain situations feel harder than they should, why certain dynamics repeat, why your responses sometimes feel disproportionate to the present moment. When you begin to trace those patterns back, you start to see that they are not random. They are responses to something that has already happened.

One of the most significant aspects of this step is the way it reframes self-blame.

Many survivors carry a persistent sense that they should have done something differently. That they should have seen what was happening, left sooner, reacted more clearly, or protected themselves in ways that now seem obvious. Step Four does not dismiss those thoughts, but it places them in context. It asks you to look at what you knew at the time, what options were available to you, and what you were trying to manage in that moment. It recognises that your responses were shaped by the conditions you were in, not by a lack of worth or awareness.

This is where honesty becomes important, but not the kind of honesty that turns into punishment. The purpose here is not to reduce yourself to your worst moments or to hold yourself accountable in a way that reinforces shame. It is to see clearly. To acknowledge where your responses have impacted your life, where you may have hurt yourself or others while trying to survive, and where you made choices that you do not yet fully understand. All of this can be held without turning it into evidence that something is wrong with you.

This step is often where people encounter the parts of their story that have been kept hidden. Not necessarily because they were intentionally avoided, but because there was no space to hold them before. There may be memories, patterns, or behaviours that you have not fully looked at, things that feel uncomfortable or unresolved. The process here is not about forcing them into the open all at once. It is about allowing them to emerge at a pace that feels manageable.

You are not required to do everything at once. In fact, trying to do so can be overwhelming and counterproductive. This work unfolds over time, in layers. You may find yourself returning to certain parts more than once, seeing them differently as your understanding deepens. You are allowed to pause, to step back, and to approach things gradually.

Some people find it helpful to make this process visible, to put it into words in a way that allows them to see what has been internal for so long. Not in a structured or formal way, but simply as a way of externalising what has been held internally. This can create a different kind of clarity, one that is not dependent on holding everything in your head at once.

What matters most throughout this step is the lens you are using. Without compassion, this process can easily become another form of self-criticism. With compassion, it becomes something else entirely. When something difficult comes up, the question is not what is wrong with you, but what you were responding to. What you were trying to manage, what you needed at the time, and what was not available to you.

This shift changes everything.

Because it separates you from the patterns you have developed. It allows you to see that these responses are not your identity. They are learned. They were shaped in specific contexts, and because of that, they can be understood, and eventually reshaped.

Step Four is not about reaching a final conclusion about yourself. It is about building a clearer understanding of how your past has shaped your present. It is about bringing what has been operating in the background into awareness, so that it no longer controls your life without your knowledge.

You are not here to punish yourself for what you find.

You are here to know yourself.

And from that place of knowing, something begins to open. Not all at once, and not in a way that removes everything that is difficult, but in a way that creates the possibility for change that is grounded in understanding rather than force.

That is the purpose of this step.

There is a point in this process where understanding needs somewhere to go. Insight on its own can only take you so far before it starts circling back on itself. Step Four is where that insight begins to take form, where what has been internal starts to become visible, organised, and grounded in something you can actually work with.

One of the most effective ways to begin this process is through resentment.

Not because resentment is the problem, but because it is often the most accessible doorway into what has happened.

It holds emotional charge. It carries memory, meaning, and impact all at once. Where there is resentment, there is usually something that mattered, something that was crossed, something that affected you more deeply than you may have allowed yourself to fully acknowledge.

Resentment gives you a place to start.

Instead of trying to map your entire life all at once, you begin with what is already present. A person, a situation, a moment that still holds weight. Something that, when you think about it, still creates a reaction in your body or a shift in your thinking. That is where the work begins.

From there, the inventory becomes less about digging randomly into the past, and more about following a thread.

You begin by naming the person, place, or situation that holds the resentment. Not in a way that exaggerates or minimises, but simply by identifying it clearly. This creates a point of focus. Something concrete to work from.

Then you name the resentment itself. What is it that you feel when you think about this person or situation? What was done, or not done, that created this response? This is not about crafting the "right" answer. It is about being honest about what is there, even if it feels uncomfortable or unfamiliar to say it directly.

From there, the process deepens.

You begin to look at how you responded to that experience. Not just in the moment, but in the patterns that followed. This is where your trauma responses begin to come into view. You may recognise ways you adapted, ways you protected yourself, ways you coped with something that felt overwhelming or unsafe. These responses might include shutting down, over-functioning, people-pleasing, withdrawing, becoming hyper-aware, or trying to control what was happening around you.

This is not where judgment comes in. This is where understanding begins.

As you continue, you begin to see how that experience impacted different parts of your life. Not just emotionally, but structurally. Your sense of self, your ability to trust, your relationships with others, your connection to your body, your sense of safety in the world. It may have affected your self-esteem, your personal relationships, your sense of security, your ambitions, your financial stability, or your ability to feel pride in yourself. These impacts are often wider than they initially appear, because trauma rarely stays contained to a single area of life.

Then, underneath all of that, there is something even more important.

The need that was not met.

Every resentment, when you follow it far enough, leads to a need. Something that should have been present, but wasn't. Safety, respect, care, honesty, protection, stability, connection. These needs are not unreasonable. They are fundamental. And when they are not met, especially repeatedly, something in you adapts to that absence.

This is where core beliefs begin to take shape.

Beliefs about yourself, about others, about what you can expect from the world. Not because you chose them, but because they were formed in response to what you experienced. When you identify the unmet need, you begin to see the belief that formed around it. The way you made sense of that absence, often in a way that placed responsibility back onto yourself.

This is the full picture.

Not just what happened, but how it moved through you. How it shaped your responses, your identity, your patterns, and your beliefs.

When you lay it out this way, something shifts.

What once felt like a collection of disconnected experiences begins to make sense as a system. A series of adaptations that were developed in response to specific conditions. And once you can see that system clearly, you are no longer inside it in the same way. You are looking at it.

That is where change becomes possible.

Not because you have forced anything to be different, but because you understand it.

And understanding is what allows you to begin choosing differently, one piece at a time.

CHAPTER 17

Step Five

Being Seen Without Distortion

"We shared our truth with a safe and trusted person who could hold it in context, without distortion or judgment."

Step Five is where something shifts from internal understanding into shared reality. It is the step where what you have begun to see about yourself, your patterns, and your story is no longer held only inside you. The purpose of this step is not simply to speak, but to be accurately seen. Not filtered through someone else's judgment, not reduced, not moralised, but understood in context.

For many survivors, that idea alone can feel confronting. Being seen has not always been safe. There may have been times where telling the truth led to being dismissed, questioned, or blamed. Times where your experience was minimised, or where the focus was shifted away from what happened to you and onto how you responded. Over time, it makes sense that you would learn to hold things in. To keep parts of your story contained, not because they are not real, but because there has not been a space that could hold them properly.

Step Five begins to undo that isolation, but it does so carefully.

This is not about telling everything to everyone. It is not about exposure. It is about discernment. Choosing who you share with matters just as much as what you share. Because not everyone will be able to hear your story in a way that supports your healing.

What you are looking for is not just someone who listens. You are looking for someone who understands what you are trying to do. Someone who can hold the full picture, who can see both the impact of what happened to you and the ways you adapted to survive it, without collapsing those two things into judgment.

This distinction is critical.

If you share your story with someone who does not understand trauma, they may focus on your behaviour instead of the context. They may interpret your responses through a moral lens rather than a survival lens. They may question your decisions, suggest what you should have done differently, or reduce your experience to something simpler than it was. Even if this is not intentional, it can reinforce the very patterns you are trying to move out of.

Step Five requires something different.

It requires a space where your responses are understood as responses, not as evidence of something wrong with you.

For example, if you have experienced a situation where your rights were overridden, where your safety or autonomy was compromised, and your response was to escalate, to become forceful, to push for accountability, that response needs to be seen in context. It is not simply about whether the escalation was "too much" or "appropriate." It is about understanding what it was connected to.

The underlying pattern may be about safety. About having your voice overridden. About a boundary being crossed in a way that activated something deeper. The escalation then becomes a response to that, an attempt to restore safety, to reassert control where it had been taken, to hold someone accountable for harm that was done.

If that response is viewed without context, it can be easily misinterpreted. It can be labelled as overreaction, as being difficult, as being too intense. But when it is seen properly, it becomes something else. It becomes a survival response that makes sense in relation to what happened.

This is what you need from the person you share with.

Someone who can see the pattern beneath the behaviour. Someone who can simplify what feels complex without reducing it. Someone who can reflect back to you not just what you did, but why it made sense at the time.

That kind of witnessing is what allows shame to loosen.

Because shame does not come from the experience alone. It comes from the way the experience has been interpreted, often through a lens that removes context and places responsibility where it does not belong. When your story is heard by someone who understands the connection between experience, response, and need, that distortion begins to fall away.

This does not mean you will feel immediately comfortable. Being seen accurately can feel unfamiliar, especially if you are used to being misunderstood. There may be moments where you want to minimise what you are saying, or pull back from it, or reframe it in a way that feels more acceptable. That is part of the process. Your system is adjusting to a different kind of response.

You are not required to share everything at once. In fact, it is often more effective to move gradually. To share a piece, notice how it is received, and allow yourself to build trust in that process. You remain in control of what you disclose, how much you disclose, and when you choose to do so.

There may also be times where the person you choose does not respond in the way you need. That is not a failure of the process. It is information. It tells you that this person may not have the capacity to hold your story in the way that Step Five requires. That does not make your story wrong, and it does not mean you shared too much. It means you need a different space.

The purpose of Step Five is not just expression. It is correction.

Correction of the way your story has been held, both internally and externally. Correction of the narratives that have shaped how you see yourself. Correction of the belief that your responses were the problem, rather than the context they emerged from.

When your story is spoken in a space that can hold it properly, something begins to shift. What once felt isolating becomes shared. What once felt confusing begins to make sense. What once felt like something you had to carry alone becomes something that is witnessed, understood, and no longer held in silence.

That is where the weight begins to lift. Not because the past has changed, but because the way it is held has changed.

Someone can sit here with me and this isn't too much. Someone can allow me to feel this for the last time, make sense of it, and witness it. Someone hears my soul's cry, and they remain beside me. Not because they have to, but because they *get it*. They haven't run away from the ugliness and left me holding it on my own. They have held it with me. They haven't fixed anything, but their presence has somehow taken the edge off.

And that is the purpose of this step.

CHAPTER 18

Step Six

Willing to Let Go

"We became willing to let go of patterns, beliefs, and protective strategies that no longer serve us."

By the time you arrive at Step Six, something has already shifted. You are no longer moving blindly through your life, reacting without understanding why. You have seen the patterns. You have traced them back. You have begun to understand how your experiences shaped the way you think, the way you respond, and the way you relate to yourself and the world around you.

You can see it now.

The ways you adapted. The ways you coped. The ways you protected yourself when you didn't have better options. You can see how those responses carried you through something you were never meant to endure, and you can also see how they have followed you into a life where they no longer fit in the same way.

And once you can see it, you cannot unsee it.

That is the part that changes everything.

Because before this, your patterns felt automatic. They felt like instinct, like personality, like something that just happened without your involvement. But now there is a separation. You can see the pattern as it forms. You can feel it as it starts to take over. You can recognise the familiar pull toward the same response.

And in that moment, something new exists that did not exist before.

Choice.

You may not always take a different path straight away, but you can no longer pretend you do not see what is happening. Even when you want to. The awareness itself creates a new pathway. One where you are no longer fully inside the pattern, but standing just enough outside it to recognise it.

That is where Step Six begins.

It sits in the space between awareness and change.

Because seeing it is one thing. Letting it go is something else entirely.

Letting go is often spoken about as though it is simple. As though once you recognise something is no longer serving you, you can just release it and move on. But what you are being asked to let go of here is not surface-level. These are not random habits you picked up along the way. These are the very strategies that helped you survive.

They are woven into your identity.

The way you anticipate, the way you protect, the way you stay ahead of things, the way you manage yourself and others, the way you hold everything together. These are not just behaviours. They are ways of being that were shaped over time, often without you even realising it.

So of course there is attachment.

Of course there is hesitation.

Of course part of you is not ready to release them.

That is not resistance.

That is intelligence.

Step Six does not ask you to force anything.

It does not ask you to suddenly become someone different, or to drop everything you have relied on overnight. The purpose of this step is much more precise than that. It is about becoming willing. Willing to see the cost of continuing to carry these patterns. Willing to recognise that what once kept you safe is now exhausting you. Willing to consider that there may be another way to move through your life that does not require you to hold everything at once.

And this is where something becomes clearer than it has ever been before.

Because now that you can see the pattern, the decision itself is no longer complicated.

You know what it looks like when it starts.

You know what it costs you when you follow it.

You know where it leads.

The confusion that once kept you stuck begins to fall away. You are no longer guessing. You are no longer trying to figure out what is wrong. You can see exactly what you have been doing, and exactly what it has been doing to you.

And from that place, the question is no longer "What do I do?"

It becomes, "Am I willing to stop carrying this?"

This is where the image begins to form.

You start to see everything you have been carrying.

Not just the experiences themselves, but the responses, the beliefs, the tension, the vigilance, the self-criticism, the regret, the shame. All of it. The weight of what happened, and the weight of how you adapted to it. It is not just one thing. It is everything that came with it, everything that stayed, everything that shaped you into the person who has been holding this for so long.

And at some point, you begin to recognise that you cannot keep carrying it in the same way.

Not because you are weak. But because it is too heavy.

This is the turning point.

Not where everything changes, but where you stop insisting that you can continue the same way.

You begin to gather it.

All of it.

The patterns that no longer serve you. The beliefs that keep you small. The ways you have had to protect yourself that now isolate you. The responses that once made sense but now create distance between who you are and who you are becoming. The energy it takes to maintain all of it, every single day, without relief.

You begin to see it as something you have been carrying, rather than something that is who you are.

And that distinction matters.

Because once you can see it as something you are carrying, you can begin to consider putting it down.

That does not mean you know how yet.

That does not mean you feel ready.

It means you are willing. Willing to stop gripping it so tightly. Willing to stop organising your entire life around it. Willing to admit that holding onto it is costing you more than it is protecting you.

There may still be fear here.

Fear of who you will be without these patterns. Fear that something will go wrong if you loosen your hold. Fear that you will lose the very thing that kept you safe. That fear makes sense.

Because for a long time, those patterns were not optional. They were necessary.

But Step Six begins to introduce a different reality.

You are not in that same place anymore. And what you needed then is not necessarily what you need now.

This is where the idea of *handing it over* begins to take shape. Not in a forced or abstract way, but in a grounded one.

You begin to recognise that you do not have to be the one who carries everything forward. That you can begin to place this weight into something that is not limited by your own capacity to hold it. Whether you understand that as God, as something greater, as the process itself, or as a form of connection that exists beyond your individual effort, the function is the same.

You are no longer holding it alone. You are no longer responsible for managing every part of it. You are allowing it to be held differently.

This is not a single moment. It is not a one-time release.

It is a process of loosening, of noticing when you pick it back up, of recognising where you are still carrying things that are no longer yours to hold. It happens in small shifts, in moments where you pause instead of reacting, where you choose not to follow the same pathway even though it is familiar, where you allow something to be different.

Each of those moments reinforces something new. That you are no longer trapped inside the pattern. That you have another option. That you can move differently now.

Step Six is not about becoming a different person. It is about recognising that the person you have been is carrying more than they were ever meant to carry, and becoming willing to set some of it down.

Not because it didn't matter. But because it does not need to define you anymore. You are not being asked to let go perfectly. You are being asked to become willing. And once you can see clearly, that willingness is no longer out of reach. Because you already know what you are ready to stop carrying.

CHAPTER 19

Step Seven

Asking to Be Freed

"We asked for support in releasing what no longer serves us, and in responding differently moving forward."

By the time you reach Step Seven, you are no longer guessing about what has been shaping you. You have seen it. You have named it. You have spoken it out loud to another human being who could hold it without distorting it. You have stood in that space of being witnessed, where the shame that once felt untouchable was exposed and did not destroy you. That matters more than it might seem at first, because it changes what is possible from here.

Step Seven builds directly from that moment.

This is where the work becomes deeply personal, and at the same time, something you no longer do alone.

Up until now, you have done the seeing. You have done the naming. You have done the telling. You have taken everything you have been carrying and laid it out in the open, piece by piece, without hiding behind minimisation or self-protection. That required humility. Real humility. Not the kind that diminishes you, but the kind that allows you to stand in truth without defending yourself against it.

And now, having seen it clearly, having said it out loud, you are faced with something simple and profound. You cannot carry it forward in the same way.

Step Six brought you to the point of willingness. Step Seven is where that willingness turns into action, not through force, but through surrender of a different kind. Not the kind that takes your power away, but the kind that releases what was never yours to hold alone.

This is where you begin to speak to God, or whatever you understand as something greater, not from a place of performance or obligation, but from a place of honesty.

Not the polished version.

The real one.

You bring what you have seen. The patterns you now recognise. The ways you respond that no longer serve you. The reactions that feel automatic but are no longer aligned with who you are becoming. The anger that overtakes you, the shutdown, the overextension, the need to control, the ways you have tried to protect yourself that now create harm or distance.

You name them. Not to condemn them, but to acknowledge them fully.

And alongside that, something else becomes clear. You also know how you do not want to live anymore.

You can see the moment where the pattern starts, and you can see where it leads. You can feel the cost of it in your body, in your relationships, in your sense of self. And because you can see it, you can also begin to recognise what a different response might look like. Not perfectly, not consistently yet, but clearly enough to know that another way exists.

This is where the request comes in.

Not as a demand, not as a transaction, but as a genuine asking.

You ask to be freed from the patterns that are no longer serving you. You ask for support in responding differently. You ask for the ability to pause where you once reacted, to choose where you once felt pulled, to stay present where you once disappeared into the pattern.

And underneath that, there is something even deeper.

You ask to be relieved of the weight you have been carrying.

The shame.

The regret.

The heaviness of what happened and how it shaped you.

Not erased, but lifted from the place where it has been sitting inside you, defining you, exhausting you, keeping you tied to something that has already passed.

This is where the idea of cleansing begins to make sense. Not in a dramatic or symbolic way, but in a felt one.

You have already done the work of bringing it into the light. You have already allowed yourself to be seen. You have already told the truth about it. That in itself is a form of clearing. What Step Seven does is take what has been uncovered and place it somewhere it can be held differently.

You are no longer gripping it.

You are no longer organising your life around it.

You are allowing it to be taken, in whatever way that makes sense to you, by something that is not limited by your own capacity to carry it.

This is where faith begins to become real.

Not because you have been told what to believe, but because you have experienced what happens when you are honest, when you are seen, and when you allow yourself to ask for something beyond your own effort. There is a quiet knowing that begins to form here. That if you are willing to bring it forward, to expose it without hiding, to ask with sincerity, something shifts.

Not all at once.

But enough.

Enough to feel a little lighter.

Enough to notice a different response where there once wasn't one.

Enough to recognise that you are not being dragged in the same way anymore.

This does not mean the patterns disappear overnight. It means they begin to lose their hold. It means you are no longer alone inside them. It means that when they arise, you have somewhere to place them, something to hand them to, rather than carrying them all the way through to the end as you once did.

There is also a growing clarity here about how you want to live.

Not just what you are moving away from, but what you are moving toward.

A way of responding that is grounded rather than reactive. A way of relating that is aligned with your values rather than shaped by fear. A way of moving through the world that does not require you to be in constant defence of yourself.

You begin to practice that. Not perfectly. But intentionally.

And when you fall back into old patterns, as you will at times, the difference now is that you see it. You bring it back. You ask again. You do not disappear into it in the same way.

That is the work. That is the shift.

Step Seven is not about becoming flawless. It is about allowing yourself to be supported in becoming different. It is about recognising that you have already done the hardest part, which was seeing, naming, and exposing what was hidden, and now allowing that to be transformed in a way that you do not have to control.

You have already been witnessed. You have already been honest. Now you allow yourself to be helped.

And in that, something begins to clear. Not all at once, but enough to know that you do not have to carry this the way you once did.

And that is what makes the next step possible.

CHAPTER 20

Step Eight

Preparing to Repair

"We became willing to acknowledge where repair may be needed, without taking on what is not ours."

Step Eight returns you to the list you have already created, but you are not looking at it in the same way anymore. Earlier, those names, those situations, those resentments were about understanding what happened to you and how it shaped you. Now, you are looking at them through a different lens. The purpose of this step is to recognise where repair may be needed, and to begin deciding what that repair actually looks like, if it is appropriate at all.

This is not about blame, and it is not about taking responsibility for what was done to you. That remains clear. What happened to you was not your fault. This step does not undo that truth. What it does is expand the picture. It allows you to see where your responses, shaped by what you lived through, may have had an impact on others or on yourself, and to consider what, if anything, needs to be addressed.

When you return to your inventory, you are not starting again. You are building on what you already know. You can see the patterns now. You can see how you responded, why you responded that way, and what was underneath it. You can see where your reactions came from, and you can see the cost of those reactions, not just to you, but sometimes to the people around you.

That does not make you the problem.

It makes the picture more complete.

There is a difference between harm and impact. Harm is what was done to you. Impact includes the ways your survival responses may have affected your life and your relationships. Step Eight is about understanding that difference without collapsing into shame.

As you move through your list, some names will be clear. There may be people you recognise you have hurt, not out of intention, but out of the way you were trying to survive. Moments where you reacted, withdrew, escalated, or shut down in ways that made sense at the time, but also had consequences. Seeing this can feel uncomfortable, but it is also where growth begins. Not through self-punishment, but through honest recognition.

At the same time, there will be names on that list where no repair is required.

People who caused harm to you do not automatically become people you owe something to. There is no expectation here that you make contact with someone who was unsafe, abusive, or damaging. There is no requirement to reopen doors that needed to be closed. Some people will remain exactly where they are, in your past, with no further action required.

There may also be people you cannot reach. People who are no longer alive, or who are no longer part of your life in any accessible way. That does not mean the work cannot be done. It simply means that the form of repair will look different.

This is why Step Eight is about preparation, not action.

You are not being asked to fix everything. You are being asked to become clear.

Clear about where repair is needed, where it is not, and where it would be unsafe or inappropriate to attempt it. Clear about what belongs to you and what does not. Clear about the difference between taking responsibility and taking on responsibility that was never yours.

This is not something you need to figure out on your own.

The person who has already witnessed you, who has heard your story in context, who understands your patterns and the way they formed, becomes important here. They are not there to judge you or to tell you what you should do. They are there to help you see the situation clearly. To reflect back where repair might be meaningful, where it might be unnecessary, and where it might be harmful to pursue.

Because sometimes what looks like something you need to fix is actually something you needed to survive.

And sometimes what feels like guilt is actually misplaced responsibility.

Having someone who can help you sort through that, who can see the pattern without reducing it, allows you to make decisions from a place of clarity rather than emotion.

This step also brings your relationship with yourself into focus.

Because as you move through your list, you will begin to see that some of the most significant impact has been internal.

The ways you have spoken to yourself, the ways you have pushed yourself beyond your limits, the ways you have ignored your own needs in order to cope or to stay safe. These are not things to judge, but they are things to recognise. Repair, in many cases, begins here.

You are not the same person who made those decisions.

You have more awareness now. More understanding. More capacity to see what you could not see at the time.

Step Eight is not about going backwards and correcting the past. It is about standing in the present with enough clarity to decide how you want to move forward. It is about recognising where something needs to be acknowledged, where something needs to be left alone, and where something needs to be approached with care and intention.

There is no rush here. No expectation that you have all the answers immediately.

You are allowed to take your time with this. To sit with each name, each situation, and understand it fully before deciding what, if anything, needs to happen next.

What you are doing in this step is creating a pathway. Not just through your past, but into your future.

A way of relating that is no longer driven by survival alone, but informed by awareness, responsibility, and self-respect.

And that is what makes the next step possible.

CHAPTER 21

Step Nine

Restoring Integrity

"We made direct amends where possible, taking responsibility for our part without explanation or justification."

Step Nine is where everything you have come to understand begins to take form in the world. Not internally, not in reflection, but in action. The purpose of this step is to restore your integrity by taking responsibility for your part, and your part only, in a way that is honest, direct, and grounded in who you are now, not who you were when you were surviving.

By this point, you already know what your part is.

You saw it in Step Four. You spoke it in Step Five. You became willing to release it in Step Six, and you asked for help in changing it in Step Seven. In Step Eight, you clarified where repair might be needed and where it would not. There is no confusion left about what belongs to you and what does not.

And that clarity is what makes this step clean.

Because this is not about going back into old dynamics. It is not about defending yourself, explaining yourself, or re-litigating the past. It is not about being understood, validated, or forgiven. It is not about balancing the scales or making everything equal.

It is about one thing.

Telling the truth about your behaviour, and making it right where you can.

Nothing more. Nothing less. There is a difference between guilt and integrity.

Guilt keeps you stuck in the past, looping over what you did, judging yourself, and often avoiding the very thing that would actually resolve it.

Integrity moves you forward. It allows you to stand in what you did without collapsing, without minimising, and without shifting the focus away from your responsibility.

This is where you name it.

Clearly. Without padding it. Without explaining why you did it in a way that softens it. Without bringing in what the other person did to justify it. You say what you did. You name the impact it likely had. And you stop there.

That is the discipline of this step.

Because the moment you begin to explain, defend, or balance it with context, you move out of your lane and back into something that dilutes the truth. You already understand the context. You have already done that work. This step is not about context.

It is about ownership.

There is also a practical side to this that matters.

If you owe something, you make it right.

If you took something, you replace it.

If you caused harm in a way that can be repaired materially or practically, you take steps to repair it. Not symbolically, but concretely. This is not about gestures. It is about alignment between what you say and what you do.

And if the harm was relational, you name it.

You acknowledge the behaviour.

You acknowledge the impact.

And if it is appropriate, you state how you intend to move forward differently.

Not as a promise to them. But as a commitment to yourself.

There is no expectation attached to this.

The other person may accept it. They may reject it. They may not respond at all. They may not want to hear from you.

None of that changes your responsibility. Because this step is not about their response. It is about your conscience. It is about removing the weight of what you have been carrying by addressing it directly, instead of holding it internally where it continues to shape how you see yourself.

You are not here to manage their reaction. You are here to make your side clean.

There is also restraint required in this step.

Not every situation requires direct contact. Some people are not safe to approach. Some situations would create more harm than repair. Some relationships belong in the past, and re-engaging would not serve you or them.

In those cases, the work is still done.

You still name your part. You still acknowledge the impact. You still make the internal correction. And you carry that forward in how you live.

Because integrity is not dependent on whether someone hears you. It is dependent on whether you are honest with yourself.

There is something that happens when you do this properly.

When you take full responsibility for your part, without defence, without justification, and without expectation, something settles. The noise reduces.

The internal tension that comes from knowing you have not addressed something begins to lift. Not because you have erased the past, but because you are no longer avoiding it.

You have met it directly.

This step is often where people realise something important.

That they are not the same person who created those patterns. Because the person who is willing to stand in the truth without hiding is already different. The person who can name their behaviour without collapsing into shame is already different. The person who can take responsibility without taking on what is not theirs is already different.

That is what restoration looks like.

Not perfection.

Integrity.

Step Nine is not about becoming someone new.

It is about becoming someone who is aligned. Someone who does not need to carry hidden weight. Someone who does not need to defend or justify their past, because they have already faced it. Someone who can move forward without dragging unresolved pieces behind them.

You do not need to do this perfectly. You do not need to get every word right. You do not need to control how it is received. You only need to do one thing.

Tell the truth about your part, and make it right where you can.

And then let it go. Because once you have done that, it no longer belongs in the same way. And neither do you.

CHAPTER 22

Step Ten

Living With Awareness and Accountability

"We continued to build awareness of our thoughts, behaviours, and patterns, and made ongoing adjustments with compassion."

Step Ten is where recovery stops being something you visit and becomes the way you live. Up until now, you have gone back, you have looked, you have understood, you have spoken, and you have repaired where you could. You have taken the weight of your past and begun to set it down piece by piece. But life does not stop moving forward, and neither do you. The purpose of this step is to make sure you do not start picking that weight back up again without realising it.

Because that is how it happens.

Not all at once, not dramatically, but slowly, through small moments that go unexamined. A reaction you don't reflect on. A behaviour you justify. A misalignment you ignore. Left unattended, those moments begin to accumulate, and before you know it, you are carrying something again. Not the same as before, but enough to pull you back into familiar patterns.

Step Ten interrupts that.

It brings your awareness into real time.

This is not about constantly analysing yourself or turning inward in a way that becomes exhausting. It is about staying connected to what you are doing as you are doing it. Noticing your responses, your tone, your reactions, your choices. Not in a critical way, but in a clear one.

You begin to feel when something is off. Not because you are overthinking, but because you are now attuned to yourself in a way you were not before. You can sense the shift. The moment where tension enters your body, where your thinking narrows, where an old pattern begins to rise. And because you can see it, you are no longer automatically pulled all the way through it.

That is the difference.

Before this, patterns ran to completion. Now, they can be interrupted.

Sometimes early, sometimes halfway through, sometimes after the fact. But even noticing it afterwards is different from before, because you do not leave it there anymore. You come back to it. You reflect on it. You take responsibility for it if needed. You make it right while it is still small.

This is what keeps things clean.

There is a discipline to this step, but it is not harsh.

It is consistent.

At the end of the day, or even in the moment, you ask yourself simple questions. Was I aligned with who I am becoming? Did I respond in a way that reflects my values? Did I slip into something old, something familiar, something I already said I was willing to let go of?

If the answer is yes, you do not ignore it.

You address it.

Promptly.

This is where integrity becomes something you maintain, not something you repair later.

If you have said something that did not sit right, you correct it. If you have reacted in a way that was driven by an old pattern, you own it. If you have crossed a line, even a small one, you bring it back into alignment before it has time to settle into something bigger.

You do not let it build. You do not let it become another layer of weight you have to deal with later. You keep your side clean in real time.

This is what stops the accumulation. Because the accumulation is what used to pull you backwards.

Not just the big things, but the small, unaddressed moments that begin to stack. The things you didn't say, the things you avoided, the things you justified. Over time, they create pressure. And that pressure is what pushes you back into the very patterns you have been working to move out of.

Step Ten removes that pressure.

Not by avoiding mistakes, but by addressing them as they happen.

There is also compassion in this step.

Because you will still have moments where you fall back into old ways of responding. That is part of being human. The difference now is not that it never happens. It is that it does not stay unexamined. You do not turn it into evidence that something is wrong with you. You recognise it, you understand it, and you adjust.

Quickly. Cleanly. Without dragging it forward.

Over time, something begins to stabilise.

You are no longer living in reaction to your past. You are no longer being pulled backwards by unresolved pieces of yourself. You are moving forward, and when something arises, you meet it as it comes. You deal with it in the moment, rather than carrying it into the future.

This is what it means to walk without baggage.

Not that nothing ever happens, but that nothing stays long enough to weigh you down.

Step Ten is not about perfection. It is about maintenance.

It is about staying connected to yourself in a way that allows you to remain aligned, even as life continues to move. It is about not abandoning yourself in small ways, the way you once had to. It is about catching things early, correcting them, and continuing forward without dragging them behind you.

This is where recovery becomes steady.

Not something you have to keep returning to, but something that is already with you. In your awareness, in your choices, in the way you move through your day. You notice. You adjust. You keep going. And because of that, the past no longer has the same pull. You are no longer carrying it. You are walking free of it.

CHAPTER 23

Step Eleven

Deepening Spiritual Connection

"We developed a deeper connection with ourselves, and with whatever brings us a sense of grounding, meaning, or spiritual connection."

Step Eleven is where the relationship you began forming in the earlier steps becomes something lived and ongoing. It is no longer just about believing that something greater exists, or being willing to turn toward it. The purpose of this step is to deepen that connection, to consciously engage with it, and to begin aligning your life with it in a way that feels steady, personal, and real.

This is where the language of prayer and connection comes in, and for many people, this is where old conditioning can surface.

If your understanding of God was shaped in environments where control, fear, or rigid belief systems were present, then this step can feel complicated at first. You may have been taught that God was something to get right, something that judged, something that required obedience, or something that existed outside of you in a way that removed your autonomy. If that is the version you were given, it makes sense that you would hesitate here. But that is not what this step is asking of you.

You are not returning to something that controlled you. You are building something new. A relationship with a higher power, as you understand it, that supports you rather than overrides you, that grounds you rather than frightens you, that connects you rather than isolates you.

This step is not about adopting someone else's definition.

It is about discovering your own.

At its core, Step Eleven is about conscious contact.

Not occasional, not accidental, but intentional. A willingness to turn toward something greater on a regular basis, not because you have to, but because you recognise that when you do, something shifts.

Your thinking slows.

Your body settles.

Your perspective widens.

You are no longer operating solely from the narrow lens of survival, reaction, and control. You are allowing something else to come in. Something steadier. Something less driven by fear. Something that can see beyond the immediate moment.

And from that place, you begin to listen.

Prayer in this context is not about asking for outcomes. It is not about trying to control what happens next or ensuring that things go your way. It is about asking for something much more grounded. The ability to see clearly what is in front of you, and the capacity to respond to it in a way that is aligned with who you are becoming.

You are asking for knowledge. Not abstract knowledge, but a felt sense of what is right, what is aligned, what is true for you in that moment.

And alongside that, you are asking for the ability to act on it. Because knowing and doing are not always the same.

This is where the relationship deepens.

You begin to notice that when you pause, when you step back from immediate reaction, when you allow space instead of filling it, something becomes available to you. A sense of direction that does not come from urgency or fear. A clarity that does not come from overthinking. A response that feels different from what you would have done before.

It may be subtle at first.

Easy to dismiss.

But over time, it becomes more recognisable.

This step also continues the process of bringing you back to yourself.

Because the more you engage in this kind of connection, the more you begin to feel grounded in your own experience. You become less disconnected from your body, less uncertain about what you feel, less reliant on external validation to tell you what is right. You begin to trust what arises within you, not because you are forcing it, but because you are giving it space to emerge.

This is not separate from your connection to something greater.

It is part of it.

Stillness becomes important here.

Not as a discipline, but as a doorway.

If your life has been shaped by survival, then stillness may feel unfamiliar. You may be used to constant movement, constant thinking, constant adjustment. Slowing down can feel uncomfortable, even unsafe at times. But it is within that space that connection becomes clearer.

Even a few moments.

Sitting.

Breathing.

Not trying to fix anything.

Not trying to work anything out.

Just allowing yourself to be present.

This is where you begin to hear something other than the noise.

Connection does not need to look a particular way.

For some, it will feel spiritual in a traditional sense. For others, it will feel more internal, more grounded in awareness and presence. It may come through quiet reflection, through time in nature, through writing, through moments where you feel anchored in something steady.

What matters is not the form. It is the function.

Does it bring you back to yourself?

Does it help you feel less alone?

Does it create space between you and your reactions?

Does it support you in responding differently?

If it does, then it is working.

Over time, something begins to change in how you move through your life.

You are no longer operating purely from instinct or from learned patterns. You are pausing. You are listening. You are asking, even if only internally, what is the next right thing here, and you are allowing the answer to come without forcing it.

This does not make everything easy.

It does not remove difficulty.

But it changes how you meet it.

There is also a growing trust that develops here.

Not blind trust, not something you force yourself into, but a gradual recognition that when you engage in this process, when you create space, when you ask for guidance and remain open to it, you are supported in ways that are different from before.

Not controlled.

Supported.

And that distinction matters.

Step Eleven is not about arriving at a fixed understanding.

It is about maintaining a relationship.

A relationship that you return to, again and again, especially when things feel unclear, when you feel pulled back into old ways of responding, when you need something that your own thinking cannot provide.

You pause.

You ask.

You listen.

And then you act, as best you can, on what feels aligned.

This is how your life begins to change in a quieter way.

Not through force, not through constant effort, but through alignment.

You are no longer trying to control everything. You are no longer reacting to everything. You are participating in your life with a different kind of awareness.

And that awareness is supported by something beyond you, something you have chosen to connect with, something that continues to meet you as you deepen that connection.

Step Eleven becomes something you carry with you. Not as a rule. But as a relationship. One that steadies you. One that guides you. And one that reminds you, again and again, that you do not have to do this alone.

CHAPTER 24

Step Twelve

Carrying the Message

"Having experienced healing, we chose to share our experience, strength, and hope with others, and to support a community of recovery."

There is a moment in this process where something clicks into place in a way that is difficult to describe until you experience it. It is not dramatic, and it is not loud, but it is unmistakable. The confusion that once shaped how you saw yourself begins to fall away, and in its place, something else emerges. Clarity. Not just about what happened to you, but about who you are, and who you were never meant to become.

You begin to see how much of your life was shaped by adaptation.

How your thinking, your reactions, your choices, your identity - were all influenced by something that was never actually you. It was what you learned. What you had to do. What you needed in order to survive. And when that becomes clear, when you can separate who you are from what you had to become, something profound happens.

You meet yourself properly for the first time.

Not the version shaped by fear, or survival, or someone else's control. But the version of you that has always been there underneath it all, waiting for the noise to quiet enough to be seen.

And when that happens, the way you see everything else begins to change.

People you once felt confused by start to make sense. Not because they have changed, but because you have.

You can see patterns now. You can see behaviour for what it is, not what it pretends to be. You can recognise control, avoidance, fear, defensiveness, projection, all the things that once pulled you in or left you questioning yourself. And you can see it without being caught in it.

You are no longer inside the pattern. You are observing it. And in that position, something else becomes available to you.

Understanding.

Not the kind that excuses behaviour, but the kind that recognises it. You can see how people are operating from their own wounds, their own patterns, their own unexamined responses. You can see the same mechanisms you once lived inside, now playing out in others, often without them even realising it.

And because you have done this work, because you have gone back, unpacked it, named it, owned your part, and let it go, you can see it clearly.

Sometimes more clearly than they can see it themselves.

This is where something else begins to rise. Not obligation. Not pressure.

But a natural pull to help.

Because you know what it took to get here.

You know what it feels like to be stuck inside something you cannot see. You know how confusing it is when everything feels wrong but you cannot name why. You know what it takes to sit with yourself, to expose what you would rather hide, to take responsibility without collapsing, to let go of what you thought you needed to survive.

And you know what happens on the other side of that.

So when you see someone else in it, you recognise it. And something in you wants to reach back. Not to fix them. Not to drag them forward. But to show them that there is a way through.

This is what it means to carry the message. Not teaching. Not preaching. Not positioning yourself above anyone else. But speaking from where you have stood. Sharing what you have seen. Offering what helped you, in a way that allows someone else to take what they need from it, without pressure, without expectation.

Because this was never something you were sold. It was something you were given. Freely. Through people who had walked the same path before you, who were willing to sit with you, to listen, to reflect, to guide without controlling, to show you what was possible simply by being who they had become.

And there is something important in that.

Because this is not something that should be turned into a transaction. This is not something to profit from. This is not something to compete over, or to position yourself through.

This is human work.

The kind of work that exists because people choose to show up for each other, not because there is something to gain, but because there is something to give. You give it away because you were given it. And because no one should be locked out of something that has the capacity to bring them back to themselves.

There is also something else that happens when you begin to do this.

It keeps you anchored.

Because every time you sit with someone, every time you hear a story that reflects where you once were, every time you recognise a pattern you have stepped out of, you are reminded. Not in a way that pulls you backwards, but in a way that keeps you clear.

You remember what it felt like to carry that weight. You remember what it cost you. You remember what it took to put it down. And in remembering, you stay aligned.

You stay connected to the path you have chosen.

Not because you are afraid of going backwards, but because you can see so clearly the difference between where you were and where you are now.

There is no requirement here to be perfect. You are not finished. You are not beyond difficulty.

But you are different. And that difference is enough.

Enough to sit with someone without judgment. Enough to recognise what they cannot yet see. Enough to offer something real, something grounded, something that comes from lived experience rather than theory.

This is how the work continues.

Not just within you, but through you. It moves forward because people carry it. Because they are willing to speak honestly. Because they are willing to show up. Because they understand that this is not about standing apart, but about standing alongside.

You are no longer surviving. You have already done that. You are living now. And in that space, there is nothing you need to protect in the same way. Nothing you need to prove. Nothing you need to compete for. There is only what you choose to do with what you have been given.

And what you have been given is something that has the capacity to change a life.

Just as it changed yours.

PART III: INTEGRATION & WISDOM

CHAPTER 25

When Triggers Come

Triggers don't ask for permission. They don't wait until you feel ready. They don't check whether you've done enough healing. They arrive—suddenly, sometimes quietly, sometimes intensely— and your body reacts before your mind can catch up.

What a Trigger Really Is

A trigger is not a weakness. It is not overreacting. It is your nervous system recognising something that feels familiar to past danger. Even if the present moment is different. Even if you are safe now.

A trigger might be a tone of voice, a look or facial expression, a certain environment, conflict or tension, feeling ignored or dismissed, a smell, sound, or memory And suddenly, your system responds as if something is happening again.

How Triggers Can Feel

Triggers can show up in different ways. You might experience anxiety or panic, a racing heart, tightness in your chest, anger or defensiveness, a strong urge to leave or escape, emotional overwhelm, or shutting down or going numb. Sometimes it feels intense. Sometimes it feels subtle—but persistent.

“This Feels Familiar”

One of the most helpful shifts is this:

Instead of thinking: **“What is wrong with me?”** You begin to recognise: **“This feels familiar.”** Because a trigger is not just about the present. It is connected to something your body has experienced before.

When a trigger hits, it can feel like you’ve gone backwards. Like all your progress has disappeared. But that’s not what’s happening.

Your body is reacting. But you are not back in that place. You are here. Now.

In the moment of a trigger, the most powerful thing you can create is: A pause. Even a small one.

This might look like taking a breath, stepping away, not responding immediately, or noticing what is happening in your body. This pause creates space. And in that space, you have a choice.

When your body feels pulled into the past, grounding brings you back.

You might try noticing your feet on the ground, naming things you can see around you, feeling the support of a chair or surface, focusing on your breath, or holding something cold or textured.

These simple actions remind your body: **“I am here. I am safe enough right now.”**

A trigger may create a strong urge to defend (fight), withdraw (flight), please (fawn) or control (freeze). These are familiar responses. But with awareness, you can begin to choose differently. Not always. Not perfectly. But sometimes. And that is where change begins.

Once the intensity settles, there is an opportunity for reflection. Not criticism. Not over-analysis. Just gentle curiosity - What did I feel? What might this be connected to? What did I need in that moment? What could support me next time?

This helps you understand your system more deeply.

Having triggers does not mean you are not healing. It means your system is still processing. Still learning. Still adapting to a new reality.

Over time, you may notice that triggers become less intense, they pass more quickly, you recover more easily and you respond with more awareness

This is progress. This is all we aim for. Progress. Not perfection. Progress.

Each time you move through a trigger with even a small amount of awareness, you build capacity.

Capacity to stay present, regulate your response, trust yourself, and feel without being overwhelmed This builds slowly. But it builds.

Triggers can be frustrating.

You might think *"I should be past this"* or *"Why is this still happening*?"

But healing is not about eliminating triggers completely. It is about changing your relationship with them. So when they come, you can respond with understanding, patience, and compassion. Instead of judgment.

You might begin to approach triggers with something like "My body is responding to something familiar." or "I can slow this down." or "I am safe enough right now." or "I can take this one moment at a time."

That is enough.

Triggers are part of the healing process. Not because something is wrong— but because something is being worked through.

Each time you meet a trigger with awareness, you are creating a new experience.

One where you are no longer powerless. One where you are present. One where you are learning to stay with yourself—even when it feels difficult.

And over time, that changes everything.

CHAPTER 26

The Promises of Recovery

Recovery does not happen all at once. It doesn't arrive in a single moment, fully formed. It unfolds.

Quietly.
Gradually.
Often in ways you don't immediately notice.

But over time, something begins to shift.

And with that shift come changes— not just in how you feel, but in how you live.

What These Promises Are—And Are Not

These are not guarantees. They are not outcomes you are required to reach. They are not conditions for success. They are possibilities. Experiences that many people notice as they move through recovery.

Not perfectly. Not constantly. But increasingly.

1. You Begin to Feel Safer in Yourself

Not all the time. But more often than before. Your body softens more easily. You can come back to yourself after being overwhelmed. You begin to trust that you can handle what arises. Safety becomes something you can access— not something that always depends on the outside world.

2. You Understand Yourself More Clearly

Things that once felt confusing start to make sense. Your reactions. Your patterns. Your emotions. Instead of asking: **"Why am I like this?"** You begin to understand: **"This is where that comes from."** And that understanding brings relief.

3. The Inner Critic Softens

That harsh voice inside you may not disappear completely. But it changes. It becomes quieter. Less convincing. Less constant. And in its place, something new begins to grow: A voice that is more patient. More understanding. More supportive.

4. You Begin to Trust Yourself

Not in a perfect, unwavering way. But in a real, growing way. You start to notice what feels right, what doesn't, when something is off, when something feels aligned. And instead of ignoring those signals, you begin to listen.

5. Your Relationships Change

You may find that you set clearer boundaries, you tolerate less harm, you communicate more honestly, you choose connection more intentionally. Some relationships may deepen. Others may shift. Some may fall away. And while that can be difficult, it often reflects growth.

6. You Respond Instead of React

There is more space. More pause. More awareness between what you feel and what you do. Not always. But enough to notice the difference. You begin to take a breath, consider your response, and choose something different - Even in small ways.

7. You Feel More Connected

To yourself. To others. To the present moment. Not constantly. But more often. Moments of calm, clarity, presence, and connection begin to appear. And they stay a little longer each time.

8. You Carry Less Shame

Shame may still visit. But it doesn't define you in the same way. You begin to see your story with context, compassion and understanding, instead of blame, harshness and judgment - And that changes how you carry it.

9. You Experience More Choice

You begin to notice you can say no, you can step back, you can choose differently, you can change your mind, and you don't need to apologise. You lose the desire to. You start to understand something more – you get a say. And more than that – what you say - goes. These choices may seem small.

But they represent something significant:

Freedom.

10. You Begin to Feel Like Yourself

Not the version of you shaped by survival. But something more grounded. More present. More real. You may not have all the answers. But you feel more connected to who you are.

11. Life Becomes More Than Survival

This is one of the most important shifts. You move from **getting through the day** to **living your life.** You begin to notice moments of joy, experience meaning, feel connection, imagine a new future. Not because everything is perfect—but because you are no longer carrying everything the same way. You're no longer surviving. You're thriving.

12. Growth Continues

Recovery is not something you finish. It is something you continue. There will still be challenges. Still be difficult moments. But you meet them differently. With more awareness. More support. More trust in yourself.

You might begin to recognise these shifts by noticing what feels different, what feels lighter, what feels more possible.

Even in small ways. That is how change happens.

The promises of recovery are not about becoming someone else. They are about becoming more fully yourself. Not overnight. Not perfectly. But steadily.

You have already begun. And as you continue, something becomes clear: Healing is not out of reach. It is already unfolding. One moment at a time.

PART IV: COMMUNITY & CONNECTION

CHAPTER 27

To the Survivor's Children

If you are the child of someone who has survived trauma, you have likely known things long before you had words for them. Not in a clear, explainable way, but in the quiet, sensory language children live in. The tension that sits in a room without being named. The shift in tone that changes everything without anyone acknowledging it. The feeling that something is happening underneath the surface, even when everything looks normal from the outside.

You would have felt it in the way your parent moved through the world. In the moments they seemed overwhelmed by something you couldn't see. In the times they were distant, or suddenly reactive, or holding everything together so tightly that it felt like it might crack. And as a child, you didn't stand outside of that trying to analyse it. You stepped into it. You adapted to it. Because that is what children do.

Children don't ask, *"What happened to my parent?"* They ask, *"What do I need to do to make this okay?"*

So you became perceptive in ways that went beyond your years. You learned to read the room before you spoke. You learned when to stay quiet, when to be helpful, when to disappear into yourself so you wouldn't add to whatever was already too much. You may have taken on a role without anyone ever assigning it to you. The one who keeps the peace. The one who doesn't cause trouble. The one who understands more than they should have had to.

And somewhere in that, without it ever being said out loud, a quiet belief can form. That your behaviour matters more than your needs. That if you can just get it right, things will settle. That being strong means not asking for too much.

None of that was ever yours to carry.

Not then, when you were trying to make sense of something you couldn't fully understand, and not now, as you begin to look back and see it more clearly. The emotional weight in that environment did not belong to you, even if you learned how to hold it.

Your parent was navigating something real. Something that lived in their body, in their nervous system, in the way they experienced safety and threat. Trauma does not stay contained in the past. It moves into the present, into relationships, into everyday moments. It shapes reactions, responses, capacity. It can make consistency difficult, even when love is present. It can make connection feel complicated, even when it is wanted. Understanding that can change how you see them. But it does not erase how it felt to be you.

Both of those truths can exist at the same time without cancelling each other out. Your parent may have been doing the best they could with what they had, and there may have been ways your needs were not fully met. You do not have to choose between compassion for them and honesty about your own experience. You are allowed to hold both.

If you grew up in that kind of environment, you may notice it still lives in you in certain ways. In how quickly you pick up on other people's emotions. In how easily you take responsibility for things that were never yours. In the way you might hesitate before expressing what you need, or second-guess yourself when something feels off. You may feel older than your years in some ways, and unsure in others. You may find it hard to fully relax, even when nothing is wrong.

These are not flaws in you. They are the imprint of an environment you adapted to. They are evidence of how perceptive you were, how responsive you had to become, how much you learned without being taught directly. They make sense, even if they no longer serve you in the same way now. And this is where something begins to shift. Because you are no longer the child in that environment.

You are someone who can look back, not to assign blame, but to understand what was happening and how it shaped you. You are someone who can begin to separate what was yours from what was not. You can start to notice where you are still carrying something that doesn't belong to you, and gently begin to put it down.

There can be a temptation, especially when you begin to understand trauma, to minimise your own experience in the process. To say, "It makes sense now, so it doesn't matter." But understanding is not the same as dismissing. You are allowed to acknowledge what was difficult. You are allowed to recognise what impacted you. You are allowed to feel what you feel without needing to justify it or compare it to anyone else's story. Your experience stands on its own. And it matters.

Healing, for you, is not about undoing your parent's past. It is about coming back into relationship with yourself in a way that was not always possible before. It is about learning that your needs are not a burden, that your voice does not create instability, that your presence does not require you to shrink.

You are allowed to take up space in your own life. You are allowed to choose differently. You are allowed to build relationships that feel steady, environments that feel safe, ways of being that are not shaped by the same patterns you grew up around. Not by rejecting where you came from, but by understanding it well enough that you are no longer unconsciously repeating it.

And there may be space, over time, for something else too. A kind of compassion that is not forced, not rushed, not demanded, but chosen. A recognition that your parent was shaped by something as well, that what you felt did not begin with you, even though it moved through you. But that always comes second.

You come first. Because this is your life. You are not here to carry what came before you indefinitely. You are not here to hold together what was never yours to fix. You are here to understand your story, to reclaim what belongs to you, and to become someone who is not defined by what you had to adapt to, but by what you choose moving forward. And that is something entirely your own.

CHAPTER 28

To the Survivor's New Partner

If you are loving someone who has survived trauma, you have likely already sensed that you are not just entering a relationship, you are stepping into something layered. On the surface, you may see someone who is strong, capable, self-aware. Someone who has done a significant amount of work on themselves. Someone who can think deeply, feel deeply, and show up in ways that are intentional and considered. There is often a steadiness there, a kind of resilience that has been earned, not assumed.

And then, at times, something else moves through.

Moments where they pull back without warning. Moments where something small seems to land heavily. Moments where their response feels bigger than the situation in front of you. Or where they need reassurance in ways that don't quite make sense if you're only looking at the present. You may find yourself trying to piece it together, wondering what you missed, what you said, what you did, or what you should have done differently.

It can feel confusing to stand in that space.

Because from where you are, you are showing up. You are being consistent. You are trying to be safe, to be present, to be someone who cares. And yet, at times, it can feel like that isn't fully landing in the way you expected it would.

What you are witnessing in those moments is not about you in the way it might feel.

But you are part of it.

Trauma responses don't begin in the relationship you are in now. They were shaped long before you arrived, through experiences that taught your partner's nervous system how to detect danger, how to respond to it, how to stay safe in environments where safety was not guaranteed. Those responses live in the body. They move quickly. They don't always pass through logic first.

So when something happens, a shift in tone, a delay in communication, a moment of distance, a misunderstanding, it may connect to something deeper than what is happening in front of you. Their response is not just about now. It is about what their system has learned to recognise, even if it doesn't consciously make sense.

From the outside, it can look disproportionate.

From the inside, it feels real.

It is easy, in those moments, to take it personally.

To question yourself.

To feel like you are being measured against something you cannot see.

You might wonder why your intentions aren't enough to settle it, why reassurance doesn't immediately land, why trust doesn't feel as straightforward as it might in other relationships. You might find yourself wanting to explain, to clarify, to convince them that what they are feeling isn't necessary.

But safety, for someone who has experienced trauma, is not built through explanation alone.

It is built through experience.

Repeated, consistent, lived experience.

Your presence matters more than you might realise.

Not in a way that makes you responsible for their healing, but in a way that shapes the environment you are both standing in. How you respond in those moments can either reinforce a sense of safety or echo something familiar from the past.

Consistency matters. Not perfection, but consistency. Being the same person over time. Not shifting unpredictably, not withdrawing without explanation, not reacting defensively when something difficult comes up. Calm communication matters. The ability to stay grounded even when something feels heightened. A willingness to listen, not to fix or correct, but to understand.

And perhaps most importantly, the ability to not take everything personally.

Because if you take their reaction as a reflection of your worth, you will begin to respond from that place. And when that happens, the dynamic can start to mirror something they have already lived through.

There are also ways of responding that can unintentionally cause harm, even when that is not your intention.

Dismissing what they feel, even gently, can land as being unseen. Telling them they are overreacting can echo a long history of not being believed. Pulling away without explanation can activate a sense of abandonment or uncertainty. Trying to push them to move on, to let go, to respond differently before they are ready, can recreate the very pressure they have spent time learning to step out of.

These things don't come from malice.

But they can still land heavily.

At the same time, it is important to understand where your role begins and where it ends.

You are not responsible for healing their trauma.

You cannot do that work for them, and trying to will only create imbalance. You can support. You can be present. You can offer consistency and care. But their healing remains theirs. Just as your wellbeing remains yours.

A healthy relationship here requires both of you.

Not one person carrying the weight of the other, but two people standing alongside each other, each responsible for their own internal world while learning how to meet in the middle.

It can be easy, especially when you care deeply, to overextend yourself. To accommodate more than you should. To step around things, avoid conflict, soften your own needs in an attempt to keep things stable. But if you lose yourself in that process, the relationship will begin to reflect imbalance rather than safety.

Your needs matter too. Your boundaries matter. Your voice matters. And the relationship will only remain healthy if both people are able to exist fully within it.

There is a particular kind of patience required in a relationship like this.

Not passive patience, not enduring harm, but grounded patience. The kind that understands that healing is not linear. That there will be moments where your partner struggles, where old patterns surface, where things feel harder than they "should" be.

But patience does not mean self-abandonment.

You are not required to accept behaviour that crosses your boundaries. You are not required to stay in situations that harm you. The balance here is not always simple, but it is necessary. What begins to build, if both people are willing, is something different.

Not perfect. Not without difficulty. But real.

Trust that develops slowly, through repeated experience rather than promises. Communication that becomes more honest over time, not because everything is easy, but because both people are willing to stay present in it. A sense of safety that is not assumed, but created, moment by moment, interaction by interaction.

You may not always see the impact you are having.

But it is there.

In the moments where they stay instead of withdrawing. In the moments where they speak instead of shutting down. In the moments where something that once would have escalated instead softens, even slightly.

That is how new patterns form.

Loving someone who has experienced trauma is not always straightforward.

But it can be deeply meaningful.

Because you are not just building a relationship in the present, you are, in some ways, participating in the creation of something that did not exist before. A dynamic that is not shaped by fear, or control, or instability, but by awareness, by choice, by care.

And if both of you continue to show up, not perfectly, but honestly, something steady can grow there. Something that is not defined by the past, even though it understands it.

Something that belongs to both of you. Something that is built, slowly and deliberately, into something safe enough to stay.

CHAPTER 29

To the Supporter

If you are supporting someone who has experienced trauma, you have likely already felt the weight of wanting to do something meaningful for them. Not in a distant or abstract way, but in a very human, immediate way. You see their pain, or you sense it even when it isn't spoken, and something in you responds. You want to help. You want to ease it, to make sense of it, to offer something that shifts it, even slightly.

That instinct comes from care. And it can also feel frustrating.

Because very quickly, you come up against something that doesn't respond the way you expect. You may say something you think is helpful, only to feel it land flat. You may try to reassure, only to realise reassurance doesn't always reach where the pain sits. You may find yourself wondering what you're missing, what the right thing to say is, how to be helpful without making things worse.

There can be a quiet pressure in that. A sense that you should know what to do. That if you care enough, you should be able to fix it.

But this is where something important needs to shift. You are not there to fix what has already happened. You are there to stand beside someone as they move through it. The difference between those two things is subtle, but it changes everything.

When you are trying to fix, you are looking for an outcome. You are looking for the moment where the pain reduces, where the situation resolves, where things return to something more comfortable. You are trying to move them out of what they are feeling. When you are present, you are not trying to move them anywhere. You are allowing them to be where they are, without adding pressure for it to change. And that is often where the real support lives.

For someone who has experienced trauma, there is often a long history of not being heard in the way they needed. Of being dismissed, questioned, minimised, or misunderstood. Sometimes directly, sometimes subtly, but enough that it shaped how safe it feels to speak openly about what they have experienced.

So when they do speak, or when something surfaces, what matters most is not the precision of your response.

It is whether they feel met.

Whether they feel believed without needing to prove anything. Whether they feel listened to without being interrupted or redirected. Whether they feel that what they are saying can exist in the space without being corrected, softened, or compared. This kind of listening can feel deceptively simple. But it is not passive.

It requires you to sit with things that may be uncomfortable. To resist the urge to fill the silence, to offer solutions, to move the conversation somewhere easier. It asks you to stay present even when you don't know what to say, and to trust that your presence itself has value.

There are moments, especially when you care deeply, where the instinct to help can lead you somewhere unhelpful without you realising it.

You might try to reframe what they are saying into something more positive. You might try to put their experience into perspective. You might ask questions that come from curiosity but land as scrutiny. You might encourage them to move on, to let go, to see things differently. None of this comes from a lack of care. But it can still land as being unseen. Because what you are doing, in those moments, is trying to change their experience rather than understand it.

And for someone who has already had their experience questioned or minimised, that can reinforce something familiar.

Support often looks quieter than we expect.

It looks like sitting with someone when they don't have answers. It looks like acknowledging what they are feeling without trying to reshape it. It looks like saying less, but meaning it more. It looks like allowing their experience to exist without needing to make it easier to hold. There is a steadiness in that kind of presence. And over time, that steadiness becomes something they can feel.

It is also important to understand that healing does not move in a straight line. There will be moments where things feel like they are improving, where your partner or the person you are supporting seems more grounded, more open, more connected. And then there may be moments where something shifts, where old responses resurface, where things feel like they have moved backwards.

This is not failure.

It is how the process unfolds.

Your role is not to push them through those moments or pull them out of them. It is to remain steady while they move through them. To not become reactive when things feel uncertain. To not withdraw when things feel difficult. To allow the process to take the shape it needs to take.

At the same time, supporting someone does not mean disappearing yourself.

It does not mean absorbing everything, or ignoring your own limits, or staying in situations that begin to impact your own wellbeing. There is a line between support and self-abandonment, and it is important that you remain aware of it.

You are allowed to have your own needs. You are allowed to step back when something feels too much. You are allowed to say no, to take space, to maintain your own boundaries. In fact, doing so is part of what makes your support sustainable.

Because support that comes at the cost of yourself will eventually collapse under its own weight.

There will be times where you get it wrong. Where you say something that doesn't land the way you intended. Where you misread a moment. Where you respond from your own discomfort rather than their experience.

This is not something to fear.

It is something to repair.

Being a safe person does not mean never making mistakes. It means being willing to recognise them, to take responsibility for them, and to adjust. It means staying open, rather than becoming defensive. It means showing that the relationship can hold those moments without breaking.

Repair builds trust.

Often more than getting it right the first time.

As you begin to understand trauma more deeply, you may start to see that what is happening in front of you is not always about the present moment. That reactions can be shaped by something older, something embedded in the body, something that is responding before it has time to think.

This understanding can create space.

Space for patience. Space for perspective. Space for you to respond in a way that is not reactive, even when something feels confusing or difficult.

Being a safe person is not about having all the answers. It is about how you show up, consistently, over time.

It is in the way you listen. The way you respect boundaries. The way you hold what is shared without using it against them later. The way you remain steady when things feel uncertain. The way you allow them to be human, without expecting them to perform healing in a way that is neat or predictable.

Safety is not something you say. It is something they *feel*.

There is also a humility in this role. An understanding that you are not leading their process. You are not directing it. You are not responsible for the outcome. You are walking alongside, offering what you can, while respecting that their healing belongs to them.

That balance matters. Because the moment support turns into control, it stops being support.

If you remain here, grounded, aware, willing to learn, willing to listen, willing to adjust, something important happens. You become part of an environment that does not recreate harm.

And that, in itself, is powerful.

You may not be able to take away what they have been through. You may not be able to change what has already happened. But you can be someone who does not add to it. Someone who does not repeat it. Someone who stands in a different way.

And sometimes, that difference is where healing begins.

CHAPTER 30

To the Child I Once Was

If I could sit beside you now— really sit beside you— this is what I would say:

Dear Little Me,

I see how hard you tried. How much you carried without anyone really noticing. How you learned to read the room before you even understood what you were looking for. How you felt things deeply, even when no one helped you make sense of them.

You weren't too sensitive. You were aware. I know you've wondered. If you were better… quieter… easier… less emotional… Would things have been different? No.

What happened around you was never yours to fix. You were a child. You were meant to be cared for—not responsible.

You adapted. You became what you needed to become to get through. You learned when to stay quiet, when to speak, how to keep the peace, how to hold things in and how to survive

There is nothing wrong with you for that. It was intelligent. It was necessary.

You were never too much. I know you felt that. Like your feelings were too big. Too inconvenient. Too hard for others to handle. So you learned to shrink them. To tuck them away.

To make yourself easier to be around. But your feelings were never the problem.

They were signals. No one taught you how to understand them. You didn't imagine it. There were moments where something didn't feel right. Where you sensed something was off. Where your body knew—before you had the words. And maybe you were told it wasn't that bad, you were overreacting, you misunderstood. But you didn't. Your instincts were there. They were just unsupported.

You were alone in ways you shouldn't have been. Even when people were around, you felt it. That sense of being on your own. Figuring things out without guidance. Holding emotions without somewhere to put them. You shouldn't have had to do that. Not at that age. Not in that way.

You deserved more. You deserved to be safe, to be listened to, to be comforted, to be understood, to be protected. You deserved consistency. Care. Attention. Not just in moments— but as a foundation.

I know what you became. I know how all of this shaped you. The strength. The awareness. The independence. The ability to read people and situations. The resilience. But I also know the cost.

The self-doubt. The overthinking. The pressure to hold everything together. You didn't choose that trade. You adapted to it.

You don't have to carry it alone anymore. You learned to hold everything inside. To manage. To cope. To keep going. But you don't have to do that in the same way anymore. You are not in that place now. You are not that powerless anymore.

I am here now. This is what matters most. You are not alone in the way you were. I am here. Not to change you. Not to fix you. But to be with you. To listen. To protect. To understand. The way you should have been met all along.

You get to be more than what you lived through. Your life is not limited to what happened. You are not defined by those early experiences. They shaped you—but they do not contain you. There is more. More connection. More safety. More freedom. More of you.

You did nothing to deserve what was difficult. Nothing. And everything you became after— was your way of surviving it.

If I could reach back and take your hand, I would. Not to pull you out of it. But to let you know: You make it through. You grow. You understand. You heal in ways that once felt impossible.

And one day— you stop trying to disappear. You come back to yourself. And you stay. And you finally learn what it is to truly love yourself, the way I do.

And I'll never leave you again.

PART V: THE ROOMS WHERE WE HEAL

CHAPTER 31

Healing in Connection

There comes a point in this journey where understanding is no longer enough.

You can know what trauma is. You can recognise your patterns. You can see your story with clarity you didn't have before. You can even begin to change how you respond. But something in you will still need more than that.

Because healing does not fully land in isolation.

It lands in connection.

Not forced connection. Not surface-level interaction. But real, human, grounded connection. The kind where you don't have to explain everything. The kind where people already understand the language of what you've lived through, even if your stories are different.

That is where meetings come in.

A meeting is not a performance. It is not a place where you arrive as your best self, your most articulate self, your most put-together version. It is a place where you arrive as you are, even if that is messy, even if that is uncertain, even if that is silent.

Especially if that is silent.

There is no requirement to speak.

There is no expectation to have insight.

There is no pressure to be anywhere other than exactly where you are.

You can sit in the room and say nothing at all, and still be part of it.

That matters more than people realise.

When you first walk into a meeting, it can feel unfamiliar.

There is often a simplicity to it that feels almost disarming. People sitting in a circle. Conversations that are honest but not forced. A structure that holds the space without controlling it. No one trying to impress anyone. No one trying to fix anyone.

And yet, something is happening.

People are telling the truth.

Not the polished version. Not the version that sounds acceptable. The real version. The version that, in most places, would stay hidden.

And as you listen, something begins to shift.

You start to hear yourself in other people's stories.

Not in the details, but in the patterns. In the feelings. In the way they describe something you've experienced but never quite had words for.

That moment, where you realise you are not the only one, is often where the work begins.

Meetings are built on structure, not to control the space, but to protect it.

There is a beginning. A preamble that sets the tone. Not as a rulebook, but as a reminder of why the space exists. A shared understanding that this is a place of safety, of respect, of confidentiality.

There is often a message to the newcomer.

Because the newcomer matters.

The person walking in unsure, guarded, possibly overwhelmed, is the most important person in the room. Not because they need to be fixed, but because they are the reason the room exists at all. Everything about the meeting is designed to make it possible for that person to stay.

Even if they don't speak. Even if they don't understand it yet. Even if they are just sitting there, trying to decide whether they belong.

There are guiding principles, but they are not enforced in a rigid way. They are lived.

People speak from their own experience. Not about others. Not as advice. Not as authority. Just as someone who has walked their own path and is willing to share what they have seen along the way.

There is no cross-talk. No interrupting. No correcting someone's story. No turning someone's vulnerability into something to analyse.

You speak when it is your turn, or you don't. And when someone else speaks, you listen.

Not to respond. But to hear.

The format of a meeting is simple on purpose. because complexity is not what helps here.

Simplicity allows people to relax into the space. To know what to expect. To not have to perform or navigate something unfamiliar every time they walk in.

There may be a reading. Something that anchors the group in shared language. Something that reminds everyone of the purpose of being there.

There may be a topic. Or a step. Or a theme.

And then people share.

Not in a structured, polished way. But in a way that is real. Usually with a very simple structure – what it was like, what happened, and what it's like now.

One person speaks, and then another. Sometimes what is said connects directly. Sometimes it doesn't. But underneath it all, there is a thread.

Honesty.

Over time, the room becomes something familiar.

Not because it stays the same, but because you begin to recognise what it holds.

You see people come in where you once were. You see them sit quietly, unsure, just listening. And you recognise that look, because you've had it.

You see people begin to speak. Hesitantly at first, then more clearly. You see the moment where something shifts for them, where they realise they can say things out loud that they thought they had to carry alone.

And you remember your own version of that moment.

There is something else that happens in meetings that is difficult to replicate anywhere else. You are seen without being singled out. You are understood without having to explain everything.

You are held in a space where nothing is demanded from you, and yet everything important is available to you.

No one is above you. No one is below you. Everyone is simply where they are. The power of meetings is not in any one person.

It is in the collective.

The shared understanding that no one here has to do this alone. That the weight you have been carrying is not something you have to continue carrying in isolation. That there is a way to speak, to listen, to reflect, to grow, without judgment or pressure.

It is quiet. But it is powerful.

And slowly, without forcing it, something begins to change.

You start to speak. Not because you have to, but because you want to. You start to recognise your patterns more clearly, because you hear them echoed back through others.

You start to feel less alone, not because your circumstances have changed, but because your experience is now shared. You start to build something that didn't exist before.

Connection.

This is why meetings matter. Not as a requirement. But as a space. A space where healing becomes something that happens between people, not just within them. A space where truth is spoken simply. A space where you can arrive exactly as you are, and that is enough. And over time, that simple truth becomes something you can carry with you.

Not just in the room.

But out into your life.

CHAPTER 32

Survivors Anonymous Preamble

The following is usually read out at the commencement of any Survivors Anonymous meeting:

"Survivors Anonymous is a peer-led recovery community for individuals who have experienced trauma, including domestic and family violence, abuse, and coercive control.

Our purpose is to create a space where survivors can come together to share their experience, strength, and hope, and to support one another in healing.

We recognise that trauma impacts the body, the mind, and the way we relate to ourselves and others. We honour the survival responses that once kept us safe, while also acknowledging that some of these patterns may no longer serve us.

In this space, we move away from shame and toward understanding.

We do not compare experiences or measure pain. We do not judge, fix, or analyse one another. We do not require anyone to share more than they are ready to. We believe that healing happens in connection.

We value safety, choice, respect, and compassion. Each person is the expert of their own experience. Each person moves at their own pace. Each person is worthy of healing."

CHAPTER 33

Guiding Values

Survivors Anonymous is grounded in a set of shared values that support safe, respectful, and meaningful connection. We refer to these values in how we interact with each other, and what we expect from others in the rooms.

Safety

We prioritise emotional and psychological safety. Participants are encouraged to share at their own pace, and to take care of themselves throughout the process.

Choice

Everyone has the right to choose what they share, how they participate, and what feels right for them. There is no pressure to speak or disclose.

Respect

We respect each person's experience, perspective, and process. We do not interrupt, dismiss, or invalidate one another.

Non-Judgment

There is no comparison of stories, no hierarchy of pain, and no judgment of coping strategies. All experiences are valid.

Confidentiality

What is shared in the group stays in the group. This creates a foundation of trust and safety.

Shared Experience

We speak from our own experience rather than giving advice. We share what has helped us, rather than telling others what they should do.

Compassion

We approach ourselves and others with care, understanding, and patience.

Accountability

We take responsibility for our own behaviour and participation, while maintaining compassion for ourselves and others.

CHAPTER 34

Opening Reading

Welcome to Survivors Anonymous.

This is a space for survivors. A space where you are not required to explain or justify your experience. A space where you are not measured against anyone else.

A space where you can simply be— as you are.

Here, we recognise that what you have been through has impacted you.

Not because you are weak. But because you are human.

We honour the ways you survived. And we gently begin the process of understanding, healing, and reclaiming.

You are not alone here. You do not have to carry everything by yourself anymore.

Take what feels helpful. Leave what doesn't. And move at your own pace.

CHAPTER 35

Closing Reading

As we come to the end of this space, we take a moment to acknowledge what has been shared.

The courage it takes to speak.
The strength it takes to listen.
The presence it takes to simply be here.

Healing does not happen all at once.

It happens in moments—
like this one.

As you leave, carry with you what feels supportive.

Leave behind what you are not ready to hold.

And remember:

You are not alone.
You are not broken.
You are not beyond healing.

We walk this path together.

CHAPTER 36

After the meeting

There is a moment, after the meeting ends, where everything goes quiet.

Not just in the room, but inside you. The words have been spoken. The stories have been shared. You've heard things you didn't expect to hear, and maybe recognised things you weren't ready to see. And now, as people start to move, as chairs shift and conversations begin again in low voices, something in you is still catching up.

You don't have to understand all of it. You don't have to agree with all of it. You don't have to know what this means for you yet.

You just have to notice what landed. Because something always does.

Maybe it was a sentence that stayed with you. Maybe it was the way someone spoke, like they weren't trying to impress anyone, just telling the truth. Maybe it was the feeling of hearing your own experience come out of someone else's mouth. Or maybe it was something quieter than that. A sense that, for a moment, you weren't alone in the way you've been alone.

You might leave here and question it. You might think, that's not me. You might tell yourself your story is different. That it wasn't that bad. That you've handled it. That you don't need this.

That's normal. Most people do.

Because recognising yourself in something like this isn't comfortable. It shifts things. It asks you to look at parts of your life you've learned to move past, work around, or keep contained. There is no pressure to decide anything now. There is no expectation that you come back. There is no requirement to believe any of this.

But if something in you felt seen, even for a moment, that's worth paying attention to. Not analysing. Not overthinking. Just noticing.

Recovery doesn't begin with certainty. It begins with a moment like that.

A small opening. A quiet recognition. A sense that something in your life, or in yourself, could be understood differently. You don't need to have the language yet. You don't need to know what steps mean. You don't need to figure out where you fit in all of this.

All of that comes later. Or it doesn't. This isn't something you force.

If you come back, you'll start to hear things differently. Not because the words change, but because you do. You'll begin to recognise patterns. In others. In yourself.

You'll notice the way people talk about things you've never said out loud. You'll hear your own thinking reflected back to you, sometimes in ways that feel uncomfortable, sometimes in ways that feel relieving. And slowly, without needing to push it, things begin to make sense.

You don't have to do anything with that straight away. You can take your time. You can sit at the back. You can listen. You can leave early if you need to. You can come and go as it feels right.

There is no performance here. No one is measuring how well you're doing this.

What matters is that you showed up.

Even if you weren't sure why. Even if you almost didn't come. Even if part of you still wants to walk away and forget it. Because something in you got you here. Not the part that has everything figured out. Not the part that feels strong or certain.

Something quieter than that. Something that recognised, maybe before you did, that something needs to change. You don't have to trust the process yet. You don't have to trust the people. You don't even have to trust yourself fully.

But if you can, just hold onto this:

You don't have to keep living the way you've been living.

There are people in that room who once sat where you are sitting. Who didn't understand it. Who didn't trust it. Who didn't think it would apply to them. And something changed.

Not all at once. Not perfectly. But enough.

If you decide to come back, you'll find your way into it. If you don't, this moment still matters. Because once you've seen something, even briefly, it doesn't completely disappear.

You don't need to rush. You don't need to decide. You don't need to become anything different overnight. Just notice what stayed with you. And take that with you when you walk out the door.

CHAPTER 37

Newcomer's Welcome

If this is your first time here, welcome.

It can take courage to step into something new— especially when you've been carrying so much on your own.

You don't need to have the right words.
You don't need to share anything you're not ready to.
You don't need to understand everything straight away.

Just being here is enough.

You may feel unsure.
You may feel overwhelmed.
You may feel nothing at all.

All of that is okay.

This is a space where you can go at your own pace.

You are welcome to listen.
To observe.
To take things in slowly.

There is no expectation placed on you.

Only an invitation:

To be here.

To begin, in whatever way feels right for you.

CHAPTER 38

Where You Stand Now

It doesn't happen all at once.

There isn't a single moment where everything clicks into place and you suddenly become a different person. No clean break. No clear line between who you were and who you are now.

It happens more quietly than that.

You're standing somewhere ordinary. Maybe making a coffee. Maybe sitting in your car. Maybe halfway through a conversation that, not that long ago, would have pulled you into something familiar. And instead of reacting the way you always have, something inside you pauses.

Not dramatically. Just enough. And in that pause, you notice it. You see it for what it is. The pattern.

It used to move faster than you.

That's the thing you didn't realise at the time. How quickly it all happened. How your body would respond before you had a chance to think. How your thoughts would follow a path you didn't question because it felt like the only one available.

But now, something has shifted. The pattern still shows up. The feeling still moves through you. The old thoughts still try to land. But they don't take you with them in the same way. Because now you can see them.

You can see the moment where you would have explained something away. The moment where you would have softened what didn't feel right. The moment where you would have stayed, just a little longer, hoping it would turn back into something it used to be.

And instead, you don't. Not with force. Not with anger. Just with clarity. There's a steadiness in that.

It doesn't feel like power in the way people talk about it. It doesn't feel big or loud. It feels simple. Grounded. Like standing on something solid after spending a long time trying to balance on something that kept shifting underneath you.

You realise, in that moment, that you're not trying to make sense of things the way you used to. You're not trying to reconcile what feels wrong with what you wish were true. You're not asking yourself to tolerate something just because you once did.

You're just seeing it. And that's enough.

There was a time when everything felt tangled. What happened to you. The way you responded. The choices you made. The ways you stayed. The ways you coped.

None of it felt clear. It felt like a series of moments that didn't quite connect, but somehow kept leading you back to the same place.

Now, when you look back, it's different. You can see the shape of it. Not as chaos. As a system.

A set of patterns that formed for a reason. Responses that made sense in the context you were in. Ways of surviving that became ways of living, long after you needed them.

And something about seeing it like that changes how you hold it. There's less blame. Less confusion. Less of that constant questioning of yourself. You don't look back at who you were and think, *what was wrong with me?* You look back and think, *of course I responded that way.* And that thought doesn't trap you.

It frees you.

Because if it made sense then, it doesn't have to define you now. You still feel things. That hasn't gone anywhere. There are still moments where your chest tightens, where something in you wants to pull away or lean in too quickly, where an old thought tries to settle in before you've even noticed it.

But now, those moments don't carry the same weight. They don't decide things for you. They don't move you in the same direction without your awareness. You have space now. Even if it's small. Even if it's only a few seconds.

It's enough. Enough to choose. And the choices don't look dramatic from the outside. They look like leaving a conversation earlier than you would have. Saying less instead of over-explaining. Not responding immediately. Not chasing something that feels uncertain. Not trying to turn something into what it isn't.

They look like you, staying with yourself. There's something else you notice, too.

The way you see other people. Not with judgment. But with clarity.

You can see patterns now. Not just in yourself, but in the people around you. The way someone avoids. The way someone controls. The way someone shifts responsibility. The way someone pulls you in and pushes you away. Things that once felt confusing now feel… readable.

And with that, something changes in how you move. You don't feel the same pull to fix it. To understand it from the inside. To stay in it long enough to make it make sense. You recognise it.

And you decide what you want to do with that. Sometimes that means stepping back. Sometimes that means saying no. Sometimes that means not engaging at all. And sometimes, it just means not internalising it.

That is new.

You realise, slowly, that you're not carrying the same weight anymore. Not in the same way. The shame that used to sit quietly underneath everything doesn't land the way it used to. The guilt that made you second-guess yourself has less hold. The constant sense of responsibility for things that were never yours begins to loosen.

It's not gone completely. But it's not running things anymore.

And for the first time in a long time, you're not trying to manage everything at once. You're not holding every outcome. You're not scanning every interaction for what it might become.

You're just… here.

In your own life.

There are still things ahead.

Still moments you'll need to navigate.

Still parts of yourself that will keep unfolding.

But you're not moving through it the way you were before. You're not moving through it blindly.

You're moving through it with awareness. And that changes everything.

Not all at once. But in every moment that follows. Because now, when something doesn't feel right, you don't need to convince yourself otherwise. You don't need to wait for it to make sense. You don't need to stay long enough to prove something to yourself.

You can see it. And you can choose.

And that is the difference between surviving something… and no longer living inside it.

THE 12 STEPS OF SURVIVORS ANONYMOUS

1. We acknowledged the impact that trauma has had on our lives, and recognised that our survival responses once kept us safe, but may no longer serve us.

2. We came to believe that there is something greater than our current state that can restore us to wholeness.

3. We made a decision to begin releasing control, and to turn our will and care toward something greater than our survival-driven thinking.

4. We explored our experiences, patterns, and beliefs with honesty and compassion, without shame or self-blame.

5. We shared our truth with a safe and trusted person who could hold it in context, without distortion or judgment.

6. We became willing to release patterns, beliefs, and protective strategies that no longer serve us.

7. We asked for support in releasing what no longer serves us, and in responding differently moving forward.

8. We became willing to acknowledge where repair may be needed, without taking on responsibility for what is not ours.

9. We made direct amends where possible, taking responsibility for our part without explanation or justification.

10. We continued to build awareness of our thoughts, behaviours, and patterns, and made ongoing adjustments

with compassion

.

11. We strengthened our connection to ourselves and something greater through reflection, presence, and stillness.

12. We shared what we have learned and supported others in their recovery.

About the Author

Tania Brown is a writer and a Specialist Trauma Practitioner based in North Queensland.

With a background in psychology and extensive experience across social system vulnerability intersections, and trauma-informed care, Tania has supported individuals experiencing complex trauma, including domestic and family violence, substance use, and systemic disadvantage. Her work is grounded in both professional practice and lived experience, giving her a deeply integrated understanding of how trauma shapes behaviour, relationships, and identity.

After navigating her own recovery journey, Tania recognised a gap in existing support models—particularly for survivors who needed more than understanding, and were ready for structured, peer-based healing. From this, she developed *Survivors Anonymous*, a trauma-informed, strength-based recovery pathway that adapts the 12 Steps to support survivors of abuse in rebuilding safety, self-trust, and connection.

Her work focuses on helping survivors move beyond survival patterns, develop self-awareness, and create lives that feel safe, meaningful, and their own. She is passionate about bridging the gap between clinical insight and lived experience, and creating spaces where survivors can be seen, understood, and supported without judgment.

Tania is the founder of **FORGED IN FIRE PRESS** and continues to develop trauma-informed recovery frameworks for individuals and communities.

Survivors Anonymous is her first book.

Made in the USA
Monee, IL
05 November 2026

67845316R00115